lothes

You co
www.
Please
Over

Is féid
www.
Muna
50c do

Class n

THE ART OF LIVING SERIES

Series Editor: Mark Vernon

From Plato to Bertrand Russell philosophers have engaged wide audiences on matters of life and death. *The Art of Living* series aims to open up philosophy's riches to a wider public once again. Taking its lead from the concerns of the ancient Greek philosophers, the series asks the question "How should we live?". Authors draw on their own personal reflections to write philosophy that seeks to enrich, stimulate and challenge the reader's thoughts about their own life. In a world where people are searching for new insights and sources of meaning, *The Art of Living* series showcases the value of philosophy and reveals it as a great untapped resource for our age.

Published

Clothes   *John Harvey*
Deception   *Ziyad Marar*
Fame   *Mark Rowlands*
Hunger   *Raymond Tallis*
Illness   *Havi Carel*
Pets   *Erica Fudge*
Sport   *Colin McGinn*
Wellbeing   *Mark Vernon*
Work   *Lars Svendsen*

Forthcoming

Death   *Todd May*
Middle Age   *Chris Hamilton*
Sex   *Seiriol Morgan*

Clothes

John Harvey

© John Harvey, 2008

This book is copyright under the Berne Convention.
No reproduction without permission.
All rights reserved.

First published in 2008 by Acumen

Acumen Publishing Limited
Stocksfield Hall
Stocksfield
NE43 7TN
www.acumenpublishing.co.uk

ISBN: 978-1-84465-150-4

British Library Cataloguing-in-Publication Data
A catalogue record for this book is available
from the British Library.

Designed and typeset by Kate Williams, Swansea.
Printed and bound by Biddles Ltd, King's Lynn.

For Julietta,
Ekaterini,
Julietta and Eleni

Contents

Acknowledgements

I want to thank warmly Cally Blackman, Alexandra MacCulloch and Sanda Miller for the expert acuity, and the helpfulness, of their comments on the manuscript of this book. Clothes are necessarily of interest to many people, and in my own thoughts on the subject I am indebted I know to very many scholars, students, friends – here I shall simply thank my Cambridge colleague Nigel Spivey for his advice on dress and undress in the classical world, and Joe Keogh of Niagara University for the fascinating pages he sent to me on Mark Twain's late love for white clothes. Above all I am grateful to my wife, Julietta Harvey, for her generosity with comments and ideas at every stage, and also for her lively insights over a longer period both into clothes and also – the two are closely tied – into life.

The incident in Stubbylee Park

One would have hoped it was an exceptional event, when in August 2007 five teenagers turned on a young couple with whom they had been chatting in a park in Lancashire, and attacked them ferociously, leaving them both with severe head injuries. The young woman never recovered consciousness and died several days later, and the young man has been left with permanent memory loss. Sadly the attack was unexceptional in our world of rage-culture: of road-rage and gang-rage, of binge drinking and binge violence. But in one respect the attack was unusual, in the UK at least. The young couple were "moshers" or goths, and the attack was provoked by their clothes.

There are countries where clothes can bring death easily. In Iraq, Afghanistan and northern India women may be killed for – among other things – wearing Western clothes rather than an enclosing gown or a sari. Those attacks may have a kind of hateful logic, because Western dress can offend ancient beliefs. But what taboo is violated by the "mosher" style? The Bible does not forbid dressing in black, or the anointing of one's eyes and nails with black. It is true that the goth style plays with death and fear, and it is possible that in the teenage killers there was a trace of fear or disturbance at the death-games played by goths. But the goth style is a kitsch take on death, and refers more to sinister characters in film than to the real dead in mortuaries. Also the goths are fit young adults, so the contrast is electric between their Adams Family "look" and their visible active youth. This makes it more cruelly ironic that a fun-play with death-fear should bring on real death. The young woman's friends came to her funeral in full goth regalia, some with plastic bats on their black-caped shoulders. So kitsch-mourning shouldered the burden of true grief.

We speak of dressing to kill, but also, in the UK now, you can dress to get killed. Fashion is everywhere in the incident. Even the way in which the young couple were injured – by stamping and jumping on their heads – follows the loathsome "style" of several recent drunken youth-gang attacks. That practice shows human mimicry in its lowest form, where it resembles a vicious infection. And the attack was provoked by fashion in its normal and – one would have said – harmless sense: fashion in clothes. The young couple were not even fully orthodox goths, the young man, Robert Maltby, has said: his girl-friend, Sophie Lancaster, had been more conspicuous for dreadlocks and piercings than for the black/white goth colour contrast. Still, they had enough of the goth style to be "moshers", and so to be killed.

The incident shows how clothes – and their implications – divide us, for the couple and the teenagers had grown up in the same town. It also indicates perhaps the intensity of fury that a style may ignite, simply because it is confidently different, even when no violence follows. The attack may also be the cruel shadow of the satisfaction, even exhilaration, that a style gives to those who wear it: the enjoyment of a bond-in-difference. Young goths together may feel that they are at *the* place where life is most special and vivid: at a cutting edge between light and dark sides. For clothes can change the face of life.

Those times when clothes may get us killed are extreme, clearly, and this book is about the normal work of clothes. But – made of soft fabric though they are – clothes have found many ways to be dangerous. Clothes have enemies, including enemies in the higher cultural realms, as well as in parks in Lancashire. I begin with the different ways clothes are thought bad, and go on to suggest how they help us: help our bodies, our being, and our discoveries of who we are and may be.

1. Why can't we trust our clothes?

They had flown the strange plane to its destination, and when they reached the city the two pilots were told they would be taken to meet the president. But the headquarters within the embassy had changed, and now resembled the upper floor of a department store, with moveable racks of men's suits. This should have been helpful, since their own clothes had shrunk to shapes of fabric joined by a lattice of threads. The pilots knew, however, that the first necessity was for each of them to ring his lawyer, who would provide his own suit to meet their needs. The first pilot's lawyer was quick to oblige. And when my turn came to ring, the phone gave a mellow whistle, which meant that my lawyer would send his suit also. But then the note changed.

At this point I was woken by the crying of a child in the house, so I never got to meet the president of the United States – who in daylight hours was the opposite of a hero for me – while the design of our extraordinary vehicle had already faded. What most interests me, however, is the role of the lawyers. Why did I need to bring them in? The night-mind partly works by puns, and presumably zigzagged from men's suits to lawsuits. But the lawyers must also have come in because they need, for their profession, to be smartly suited: not cheaply, or we might doubt their success, and not too richly, or we would fear their fees. In style they must not look like fashion victims, nor like fashion exiles. Because of the role clothes play in the world, a lawyer's suit for an important case may give us a reliable model to fall back on – if we are suddenly stripped naked on the eve of an important meeting.

At all events the dream was much about clothes – losing them and getting them – and this perhaps reflects the way that clothes matter to us. We may think of them as an outer surface, a husk or soft armour, but our dreams show that our clothes are inside us as well. In our dreams, indeed, they may destroy us, for instance if they suddenly vanish. In life too we may depend on them. They cover our shyness about our bodies, and our shyness about who we are. They can spring bad surprises on us, if we are suddenly made to feel in company – by a tactless remark or, even worse, a tactful one – that some item we are wearing is absolutely wrong both for us and for the occasion. Then for some moments our worth hangs on a "surface" mistake we have made, as bad as a wrong act or as a cruelly wrong thing said. Bad clothes do not, as bad words may, slip quickly into the past. They haunt us in the sight of everyone until we can get out of them. The mistake we made in choosing them is not itself a garment that we can take off; it has revealed a flaw in us.

Clothes, in other words, can be treacherous companions, perhaps the more so because they touch us closely, because they touch our skin. Their betrayal of us is like betrayal by a sibling, and siblings too can be treacherous companions. And if one looks at large through history – at the way clothes have been represented by thinkers, poets, even artists – one finds a recurring mistrust. I want to examine this mistrust, because it seems to me there must be a further reason for it, beyond the faults that clothes commit. Since clothes are such an ambiguous quantity, it seems better to approach them from a distance, warily, rather than to start inside the wardrobe and then walk slowly from it.

It is not surprising, of course, if new fashions cause dismay. They certainly mean to cause a stir. And fashion may exaggerate to make its point. There was naturally some mockery in the late-sixteenth century when the "cartwheel" ruff became so wide that people's heads looked like puddings on plates. Nor is it surprising if public moralists have denounced sudden plunges of the neckline, high-rises of false hair or beauty-spots scattered like an epidemic. What is surprising is that clothes in general, clothes of all sorts, have provoked mistrust in the wisest of men. In philosophy, for instance, clothes have a negative value. We wear them but they are not us: the important "us" is hidden by them. Wittgenstein said that language disguises thought as clothes disguise the body. Less severely, Kierkegaard said that as one takes off one's clothes in order to swim, so one must strip oneself mentally naked in order to know the truth. This may be true, and Kierkegaard sees clothes more as an impediment than as a disguise, but still his attitude to dress is negative. Schopenhauer said that attending too much to the thoughts of others was like wanting to wear someone else's old clothes. He has little to say about new clothes, or about his own clothes. And if one turns from what philosophy has said about clothes in general, to what philosophy has said about fashion, the severity is extreme indeed. Thoreau famously said, "Beware of all enterprises that require new clothes", and Kant had said "fashion belongs under the heading of vanity ... and also under the heading of folly". When Kant says this, of course, he sounds remarkably similar to the popular moral critics of fashion whom I mentioned before, perhaps illustrating what the philosopher F. H. Bradley said: that philosophy is common sense in a dress suit.

Western philosophy has long had a derogatory take on clothes, to the effect that since Truth is naked, clothes are likely to be lying. The idea perhaps goes back to Plato, for whom all appearances were a false front hiding an unseen truth. It is not that good things have never been said. Erasmus said that clothes were "the body's body", and the thought is full of suggestive subtlety, if the various relations between clothes and the body are compared with the relations between body and soul. A later philosopher, Martin Heidegger, was not always happy in his own use of clothes: through the 1930s he increasingly dressed like a Bavarian peasant in a way that chimed with his National Socialist sympathies. But he also recalled that, when he discussed the translation of ideas between German and Japanese, his friend Count Shuzo Kuki sometimes "brought his wife along who then wore festive Japanese garments. They made the Eastasian world more luminously present, and the danger of our dialogues became more clearly visible" (Heidegger [1959] 1971: 4). The clothes showed, as words could not, the reach of the differences that exist between cultures, because not merely Countess Kuki but "the Eastasian world" was "luminously present" in her clothes.

There is perhaps no surprise that moralists in the Christian era have been suspicious of clothes, since, in the perspective of the Bible, clothing was implicated in the fall of man. According to Genesis, Adam and Eve lived naked in their garden of plenty until they ate the fruit they had been told not to eat, and became ashamed to see their bodies. From the leaves of the trees they made themselves aprons, or breeches – in different translations – to hide the parts they should not show. They hid themselves away, too, from the voice that came after them, and when they shyly emerged their clothes of sewn leaves were the proof and sign of their guilt and shame. But one cannot un-fall. They were packed out of paradise, and God himself, taking pity, gave them animal skins to wear, in addition to the leaves that doubtless were as perishable as many later fashions.

God's decision to clothe them in the raw form of leather – protective and durable in the fallen world – shows that the divine view of clothing was not one-sided. And if one travels to the other end of time, dress values are reversed. Revelation makes clear that at the second coming the blessed and the saved will be robed – like the angels and the risen Christ – in white. In hell, on the other hand, according to the images of Western art, the damned, writhing in pits of sulphur, will be as naked as Adam and Eve had been in paradise. So too may be the demons – although they are likely to have scales – and so too may be Satan. It is easy to see why the damned should be naked: so as to be both exposed, and denied all protection. And as to the style of dress in heaven, there should perhaps be no comparison between those pure and presumably never changing robes and the short-lived fopperies of human fashion. The robes of heaven conform to an ancient dream that an ideal being would be both radiant and clothed in light. The white clothes of heaven are presumably woollens – whiter than any fuller could whiten them, we are told in Mark's account of the Transfiguration. The cleanest, finest, whitest of wools had been for some millennia among the most precious and luxurious forms of human clothing: it is fitly worn in the domain of the Lamb.

The position of the Bible on dress is, in other words, more complex than the simple association of clothes with the Fall. And if one moves from pictures of hell to the happier visions of Western art, it is clear that painting differs from philosophy in having a more divided attitude to clothing. The masters of the Renaissance loved to render the lustre of ample, deep-coloured satins and velvets. And in terms simply of square inches of canvas, the ravishing painting of quality clothing has been a significant part of Western art. This is again not surprising, seeing that a part of Western art has been an icon-factory for the rich. And painters themselves have shown some suspicion of dress, and especially of luxurious dress. When he painted *Sacred and Profane Love*, Titian represented sacred love by the beautiful bare body of an active-looking young woman, while profane love wears a fashionable dress, and has a stolid indoor look. In any case one might expect a visual artist to prefer a lovely naked body to a body that is wearing robes, however sumptuous they may be.

If one moves again, from visual art to literature, one finds still a mistrust of clothes, although with a different emphasis. Time and again Shakespeare and his contemporaries will contrast fair but false appearances – gorgeous clothes, in other words – not with hidden truth, but with the hidden corruption of the wearer. "Robes and furred gowns hide all", cries King Lear. Earlier, like Kierkegaard, he has begun to take his clothes off, since he too wants to gain the truth. He shouts at his clothes, "Off, off you lendings". It is true that King Lear also pities "poor naked wretches": he sees that the naked do need to have clothes.

Human dress, in the traditional wisdom, seems often to be caught in some bad act. Clothes cannot win: either they show what should not be shown, or they hide vice or they hide the truth. Actually it is not clear why Truth needs to be naked. If we were not so prejudiced against clothes, we would not need to emphasize that Truth does not wear them, any more than we need to emphasize that Truth is not whistling, or not driving a car. There may be, in the prejudice, a gender twist. Poets, painters and philosophers used mostly to be men, and it is well known that women have been much concerned with dress. When Socrates recommends either no clothes, or the simplest clothes, in Plato's *Republic*, his annoyance with current styles is directed especially at articles "that have to do with women's adornment". Even novels by women novelists, such as Jane Austen and Elizabeth Gaskell, will mock women in general for their tittle-tattle about the latest bonnets and ribbons, and both in novels and in life a dandified man is often thought effeminate. More recently, the philosopher Friedrich Nietzsche has said, "Comparing man and woman in general one may say: woman would not have the genius for finery in general if she did not have the instinct for a *secondary* role" ([1886] 2003: 102). A similar attitude informs some neo-Freudian thought in the idea of the masquerade, according to which the performance of womanly identity, including the priority given to clothes, is conditioned by anxiety about the absence of a phallus. So, to reassure both men and women, the glamour show is mounted.

Since women in many cultures are interested in adornment it is fair to look for fundamental causes, but still it is risky to equate adornment and showy dressing with femininity (and with the status of a real or metaphorical phallus). One odd corollary of doing so would be the idea that ruling classes are feminine. So, if we time-travelled to the French eighteenth century, and stood a peasant beside an aristocrat, we could think the active, loud-voiced peasant in his big trousers the male phallus in person, while Monsieur le duc, with his powder and beauty-spots, skipping to a minuet in a wide-skirted coat of flower-patterned satin damask (with matching satin "culottes") must be the lady. Monsieur le duc does, however, wear something further: that traditional dress-accessory of menswear, a sword. Not a symbolic or phallic sword but a real blade, possibly blooded from duelling. And when not bowing with grace on the parquet of Versailles, he might at some point lead a cavalry charge against a cannonade, where his gold braid would make him a conspicuous target. Then he might seem the man while the peasant in his big smock, fenced in by domesticity, bent to his loom in the front room of the cottage when not milking goats in the field behind it, would seem the housewife. To answer Nietzsche, then, it seems odd to argue that the peacock aristocracies of the world, who undoubtedly had "the genius for finery", also had "the instinct for a secondary role".

As to the taste for adornment and "finery", it clearly belongs to the social theatre, and flourishes in lifestyles of enforced idleness. A similar premium on appearances has operated in some periods for lords and ladies, and at other times for the leisured wives – but also for the leisured sons – of the rich. But in all such discussions, what is also interesting – whether we are Socrates or Kant or Nietzsche, or other people again entirely – is that when we talk about clothes in a general way, we tend to push them away from us, into the realm of the suspect or the realm of the feminine. It is as if we felt crowded by the clothes we wear, or had become claustrophobic being cooped up inside them, and yearned to have an envelope of clear space around us, to stand between our naked bodies and cloth.

Not all important thinkers, it must be said, have been brief and disparaging on the subject of dress. On the contrary, in the past two centuries some important writings have been addressed to clothes: works by the historian Thomas Carlyle, the economist Thorstein Veblen, the sociologist Georg Simmel and the semiologist Roland Barthes. But even in these works the attitude to clothing may be nearly as critical as that of the philosophers, although more subtle, certainly. I shall mention these arguments because they do make a small tradition of clothes philosophy. It is, to say the least, a sceptical tradition.

The *Sartor Resartus* of Carlyle, for instance, has a real feeling for the weave and the fibre, as it were, both of fabrics and of fashions. But still his main point about clothing is both metaphysical and negative. He argues principally that the existing forms of church and state are sorts of old clothes of the soul, and should be thrown out for life to advance. His interest, not unnaturally, is rather in the new life of church and state than in any new style of clothing as such.

Veblen argued, in *The Theory of the Leisure Class*, that the principal purpose of those who bought expensive clothes was to show off their wealth by wasting it. This task was delegated especially to the idle wives of the rich. And how better could a man display his success than by flaunting a trophy wife, with a beautiful, willowy, strengthless body, idle and shimmering like a jeweller's window? Beautiful clothes come off badly here, and Veblen reinforced his argument by buying his own clothes by mail order from a Sears and Roebuck catalogue: clothes of stiff, honest, canvas-like stuff, which, his friends said, stood up by themselves whether or not he was in them.

Simmel, the German sociologist, was different: he was a charismatic public speaker noted for his elegance. His essay "The Philosophy of Fashion" is filled with subtle insight, although he is clear that fashion is "a playground for dependent natures". For

Simmel, clothes are evanescent weapons within the class war. Those rising will try to mimic the dress of the rich, who in turn will change style to avoid their imitators. So you get fashion, and the changes of fashion. Simmel's argument, like Veblen's, must have had much truth, although it covers less ground in our world, where trends are set not by old money but by new celebrities, who do not mind if their high-price designer outfits are mimicked in affordable high street versions.

Oddly enough, Barthes, in his fullest study, *The Fashion System*, is not strongly interested in reading clothes for their political meaning. He shows how garments, photographs and snatches of prose cooperate to make a fashion language. But fashion he treats as a wild card, descending on some items and not on others in an arbitrary and fortuitous way. His view sorts rather easily with Kant's view that fashion is vanity and folly.

With friends such as these in the serious intelligentsia, clothes scarcely need enemies. And these critical readings have force: clothes, for all their softness and give, will undoubtedly reflect the cruel politics of wealth. But that is not all that may be said of clothes, and what is missing from the accounts given by philosophers, moralists and theologians, and also by the accredited large thinkers on clothing, is an adequate description of the way in which our own clothes are helpful to us in the daily business of life when we are not flaunting wealth and class. Also largely missing from the authorities I have mentioned – except for the painters – is due recognition of the *art* of dress: of the fact that, whether they are expensive or bought for a bargain price, clothes can be attractive, a true find, a delight to wear and see.

It is not that the important thinkers allow no visual charm to clothes. But they give the "aesthetic" dimension such a subsidiary recognition that the value of it seems close to nil. Simmel places clothing in the "applied arts" like interior decoration. He himself dressed elegantly, but his own clothing choices are scarcely mentioned. That may be his modesty. But there is a curious effect that often occurs when an author begins to write about clothes: he comes to speak of clothes as though always they are worn by other people. Of course, when we look at the clothes that other people wear – and when we look at the "other" people who wear them – then it is not hard to see the vanity, the showy waste, the social mimicry. And those things are real. But still, caught up in their impassioned critique, the clothes authors will hide their own clothing habits as they would their nakedness. Or rather they write about clothes as though they themselves neither wore clothes nor went naked. They place themselves in the unimaginable. Viewed in this light, the widespread mistrust of clothing becomes, I think, more interesting. It is as if it were important to us to show our independence: our independence from clothes, and from our own clothes. But this denial would only have such importance if after all our dependence were great: if the denial touched, or covered – or clothed – the most sensitive part of us.

***

I want to go on, in the following chapters, to look at ways in which clothes are important to us. But before doing that I had better allow that, yes, there *are* reasons why one might take against clothes. Clothes may be a disguise, or a form of hypocrisy – if one dresses like a scrupulous public servant, say, while secretly one is on various forms of take. Also fashions, especially extravagant fashions, may be ridiculous, and vain and foolish. There is also the whole question of social status, and the work that clothes do as status symbols, which is not in itself attractive. Clothes may use their expensiveness like a weapon. Clothes perhaps converse between themselves, in the accents of an exclusive society. The smartness of smart clothes says, "Respect me". But if clothes assert, they flatter too, and the smartness of smart clothes also says, "Look, I show my respect for you by taking the trouble to dress so well". The offer is reciprocal: clothes show respect but also seek respect. Clothes may be metaphors for our own feelings, but also they may be wishful metaphors for the feelings we want other people to have for us. This is natural enough, but it may also be done with pompous solemnity. Very smart clothes may have their own way of holding coldly aloof from us.

Again, a problem may arise for smart clothes if they meet casual clothes *en route* for the same occasion. At once they converse, even if the wearers say nothing. For the casual clothes ask, "Why have you taken so much trouble? Why so up-tight? Who is it you are anxious to impress?" To which the smart clothes may disdain to reply. Clothes have various ways of manifesting social competitiveness, and the show clothes of the idle rich – and even more of their spoilt children, drunkenly falling out of sharp cars in Kensington – can be hard to take. For clothes can be truculent, and cooperate with the wearer in performing an indifferent scoff at everyone. Then perhaps one says, "We're in Europe now – let's have the guillotine over here". And if wearing goth style can bring on murder, it may very well be that in the French Revolution the iridescent silks of the *ancien régime* did help to whet the blade that hung above their plump pink powdered lace-frilled necks.

In other words, if clothes are signs that cry "status", they also work like targets for those deprived of status. And perhaps in the whole critique of clothes, it is the status that clothes signify that is especially resented. For the examples that clothes critics give of bad clothes, and hypocritical clothes, and disingenuous clothes, are normally taken from luxury clothes. But should all clothes be blamed for the bad performance of exclusive items? For we all wear clothes, and may well think there is nothing bad about our own clothes.

Yet our own clothes, too, may not be innocent, for there is another shadow again on very many clothes: on those of the rich and of the not so rich. I say shadow since it cannot be called a stain, for if clothes are all show, this is the feature that does not show.

There are people who stand on the far side of clothes, whom we never shall see however closely we stare into the fibres: the people who wove and stitched and made them, working perhaps in low-lit rooms for less than starvation-pay. We cannot see the sweatshop through the shirt. This is not an issue that has detained philosophy greatly, although it is an issue that does weigh now with many people. So it should, for if conditions were hideous in the "satanic" mills and sweatshops of the past, still conditions were not then necessarily worse in sum than they are now in Honduras or Haiti or Bangladesh or Indonesia (or again in sweat-cellars nearer home, in London, Los Angeles, New York) – now that modern communications, and modern commercial initiatives, have made the poor of all the world the workforce of our high street chains.

In many cases the connection is indirect, since the retail outlet buys from a "manufacturer", who subcontracts to the actual suppliers, who buy directly from the sweatshops and the home-workers. But the connection may also be direct: retail entrepreneur Philip Green is famous for being quick off the mark in getting clothes made for nearly nothing in China, and Gap is supplied directly by the Mandarin works in El Salvador, where conditions have been extremely harsh. By such thriving initiatives the differential opens between the high street chief executive getting between two and three million a year, and the villager in Bangladesh working for 13 pence an hour, or his children working for less and with damage to their sight. At the root of the inequity is the fact that many of the actions that go to making clothes do not require expensive training or equipment: the poorest of us can stitch. This is not invisible mending, but invisible making, although fortunately, thanks to groups such as War on Want, the inequity is becoming visible, and even hard to hide or hide from. There has been movement at higher levels. In 1997 the Clinton administration established the White House Apparel Industry Partnership, and more recently our own main chains, alert to bad publicity, established the Ethical Trading Initiative. To date,

however, there has been scarcely any effective legislation, and virtually no effective enactments of codes of conduct. The situation at the
sewing machine remains as miserable as it has ever been.

It is possible that matters may one day be assisted by a further
element in the transaction: the brand name or label of the big
sellers and suppliers. Our society, and our economics, are much
into brand names, and on clothes the brand names are now worn
on the outside, not printed small on a sewn-on label, but blazoned
across the chest. Branding is questionable from many points of
view. Names are easily forged, or stolen. In the endless Sunday
street market in Piraeus, in Athens, I recently saw three piles of
identical black boxer shorts bearing, side by side in big letters, the
names "Calvin Klein", "Calven Klain" and "Calven Kiein"; the prices
were the same, and whether even "Calvin Klein" was Calvin Klein I
do not know. But although the name may be copied or stolen, the
original firm will be a strong performer, and often a monopolistic
monster, since its label power can squeeze out of existence small
productions with other names. So the mere name of a talented individual becomes in time the giant banner of a devouring corporate
beast: an ogre that, like the maker, we scarcely see when we queue
to buy a three-pack of underwear.

Brands *are* so formidable because, perhaps weakly, we let
ourselves count on them. A brand name, a label, saves us worry;
it even saves us thought. It also serves as instant fashion: if we are
wearing Armani – from the expensive, not the high street range –
then we *are* fashion, we are chic in person, as if all we really needed
to wear was the label itself, like a big sandwich-board. And yet even
the super-labels are vulnerable. A "reputation for excellence" can
be lost as well as won. True, change either way is like getting an
oil tanker to turn a corner. But change occurs: the meaning of the
label can change from "excellence" to "expensive plus dull". Slowly
sales fall and profits wilt. Labels are vulnerable to scandal also.
Because they are so big, news about them makes headlines; and

headlines can hurt even them, especially if reinforced by photos of the workforce, lean, bent down, visibly starving as they slave. Then it may be, reluctantly, with bleeding profits, that the label for excellence seeks tardily to make an honest label of itself. The Mandarin works in El Salvador did improve its conditions when its conditions became public. But there is something quixotic also in resting too much hope in headlines and boycotts. As noted, it is not clear that conditions all in all have changed much. Not that clothes are the only items in our shops to have such a shadow over them: many consumer desirables, from toys to electronics, are as bad.

There are, certainly, suppliers on the internet who practise fair trade principles although there is no general application of fair trade to clothes (and the Fairtrade Foundation itself does not yet certify clothes). From the People Tree website one can order "garments that are beautiful, as well as caring", from T-shirts to yoga wear. All the details of their making are given, back to the villages where the cloth is hand-woven. And from the earliest days of Margaret Thatcher, polemical designers such as Katharine Hamnett have spoken from T-shirts, saying "Clean Up or Die" and "Choose Life" (before the Pro-Life lobby tried to hijack the phrase). But the volume of such off-trend business must be tiny compared to high street flows.

Moral philosophy, it seems, has two distinct faces as far as clothes are concerned. "Morality", as to clothes, means decency of covering, while "ethics" means the politics of exploitation. The ethics of clothing has many twists: nearly as many as life itself, since nearly all that we do we do wearing clothes. There is famously the issue of furs – fur coats, muffs, fur hats – and the quantity of small mammals that need to perish to keep a "rich bitch" in furs. The pro-fur lobby has recently retorted that at least its products are natural; all furs, in that sense, are green. This is an argument to make one grimace, but the issue itself is not in fact simple, since there are peoples living within the Arctic Circle, such as the Inuit, who live by skinning and curing skins, and naturally wear furs all year round.

They too were reduced to near-starvation economics at the height of the anti-fur campaign. And then again one would pull a wry face if one heard a "rich dog" say he had bought his dame a luxury fur in order to help the Inuit.

But the ethics of clothes needs a book or books itself, and an author more qualified than I am in ethics, law and economics. The present book is more general. I must acknowledge too – to turn to the positive – that if clothes have hidden guilts and shames, they have also been identified, sometimes, with the precious values of life. The philosopher George Santayana included clothes among those artefacts that may have beauty, and before beauty, he argued, one is in "the presence of something good" ([1896] 1961: 33).

I shall come to the good in clothes. In the meantime, to make up for what has been said against them, I shall close these opening remarks by noting the ways in which clothes can matter *very* much. Not our own clothes, for our vanity may be tied up in them, but the clothes of other people, who may also be dear to us. I am thinking, for instance, of my eldest grand-daughter, when she was three, as I remember her and also see her, in a late afternoon photograph on a sunny beach in Greece, looking into the distance with a vulnerable, bright smile, and wearing a very light, very thin cotton dress. The material has a crumpled texture, with wide, fuzzy-edged stripes of pink and light turquoise running from top to bottom, with white stripes in between. It is a nothing of a dress – its weight must be zero – and she couldn't get into it now: it is folded in a drawer waiting for her sister. But she was happy with its delicacy and nice-ness: that she is wearing it means that we were leaving the beach. And her look then, and the dress, and that place at that time, are bound or fused for me at the sharp end of beauty – the cutting edge, one could almost say.

Of course we hugely impose on children, who cannot buy their own clothes. We say, "Oh you do look pretty in that!" Then we are not sure how responsible we are when children like their clothes.

It is true there is also a world of children's fashion, making money for someone, which causes little girls to like pink too much. I am not concerned to trace responsibility, however, but to isolate an area where clothes may move us with a delight close to love. Then the feeling for the garment is a feeling for the person, but still the garment has its identity. As to that summer dress, its warmth and protection value is nil, and its durability and price are probably small. But it hung light and easy, and moved very gracefully each time its wearer moved, while the pink and light turquoise have that lively vibration that complementary colours always give.

I have chosen my grand-daughter because I would seem uxorious if I mentioned my wife, and how much I liked the knitted dress with thick black and coffee-coloured stripes running round it – horizontal stripes with thinner white stripes between – that she often wore when I first used to notice her in the university library at Cambridge, seeming always, as she perused a book, or chatted to someone else in the tea-room queue, to have something inside her that amused and pleased her, and contributed to her glow. But personal remarks will seem sentimental. I shall take refuge in a classic. One of the stories, woven through the fabric of Tolstoy's *War and Peace*, concerns the Old Prince. He lives alone in the country with his unmarried daughter, Princess Mary, who is to marry, at the novel's end, one of the male leads, Nikolai. Relations between father and daughter are strained, partly because of the exorbitant demands the ageing tyrant lays on her, and at times the reader may be reminded of Shakespeare's old King Lear being tetchy with his daughter Cordelia. Both authors faced the problem of how best to crack an entrenched aged wilfulness, so that father and daughter may come together again. In Shakespeare Lear raves, exposed on the heath, and strips off his clothes in a raging storm; clothes are always important in Shakespeare, as we know from Hamlet's black. In the end Lear sleeps – a healing sleep – and wakes into tender recognition of his daughter.

Tolstoy disliked *King Lear* and he does things differently: he makes the Old Prince have a stroke. This sounds an unglamorous option, especially when Tolstoy describes, painfully well, the ugly awkwardness of the old man's efforts to speak to his daughter. She cannot understand his muffled noise, while he starts to cry, like a child, with frustration. It is only later that she realizes why she had misheard him: it was because she had expected him to say the kind of peremptory thing that he always used to say. But the stroke has got his ego out of the way. He is different now, and she finally realizes that what he has been trying to say is "Put on your white dress, I like it". When she realizes this, she herself bursts into tears; a little later, he has another stroke, and dies. We are not told precisely why he liked the white dress; it may be he liked its innocence, and the effect would have been different if he had said, "Put on your red dress". In any event, the words are simple and central. They speak from and to the heart of love in father and in daughter: and they manage a loving reconciliation simply by naming a dress.

2. On trend, off trend: fashion and freedom

We have divided feelings about our clothes, and there is an ambiguity in clothes themselves. In proverbs and stories they are dangerous things. A harmless-looking sheep may be a wolf inside sheep's clothing. Even grandma may be a wolf, hidden within grandma's nightclothes and bedclothes. In such stories, however, it is not the clothes that are at fault. For the stories are not really about clothes, they are about human behaviour. They say that people may be ravenous to use us when they seem to be all sweet smiles and care. It is true that clothes make a good metaphor for hypocrisy, just because they are so close to us, so like a skin. But still they are not us: they are something we "put on", as we also "put on" a performance.

Actually, clothes are not great hypocrites, in spite of the proverbs. They may deceive us at first, but as we talk to the person within them it needs only an odd phrase or an uneasy smile, and the smart suit or borrowed uniform, or even the misleading tie, starts to be suspect. They cease to deceive. Then it is the voice that is most like a disguise, while we search, inside the smile, for a glint from the teeth of the crocodile.

Clothes, in other words, are not bad in themselves, and they have at best a supporting role in assisting bad acts and deceptions. Their role in general is to assist. They may contribute to bad performances, but also they may help us in what we feel are important ways. If we ask what clothes *do* for us, the perspective changes, from the view that we get if we look at clothes from the outside. Of course clothes *are* the outside: they are the outside of people, and clothes in the mass are the outside of society. But also we are inside the clothes, and there is a point in asking how clothes look from the inside.

To see them from the inner angle, one must turn to a different kind of clothes writing – for instance, to the readers' letters that sometimes appear in the fashion pages of magazines. Those who write in are anxious. They ask "*What* shall I wear?" not "How shall I achieve a conspicuous waste?" They ask how they may look good, not how they may cause people to think that they are only travelling by tube because their stretch-limo is gridlocked. They are asking clothes for help, because looking good is not always easy. But although they want to look good, the writers also want to be, visibly, themselves, which suggests that there is an issue of integrity present.

Presumably the anxiety that is voiced in the letters is shared by other readers who do not write in. There are, if one adds them up, several hundreds of fashion pages, across different publications, appearing in the newsagents each month. The pages, mostly, are non-committal: they are mainly made up of photographs of attractive models in an endless range of outfits. They have hiccupping captions made up of websites, phone numbers and price tags: "pencil skirt £210 by Anne Valerie Hash, black bra, £20 from thegirlcanthelpit.com". It all looks very shop-window, very market, with free advertising for the boutiques and designers under the guise of customer advice.

One may speculate about tie-ins between shops, editors and publishers. But the other side to these pages is that they consist of answers: answers to the unasked questions (except when they *are* asked in readers' letters) "What shall I wear? How should I look?" In popular magazines the models meet our eyes, sometimes blankly, sometimes cajolingly, but essentially as friends. For they are there to guide us, by tactfully sorting and trying on the clothes that are available, and standing where they are brightly lit so that we can see them well. The fashion columns likewise – which are very short nowadays – consist essentially of advice and warning, in the guise of entertaining remarks. If you're busty you should go for a waisted design to maximize your curves, but avoid large lapels – they add pounds on top. And if you're a pear shape, cinch in your waist with a wide leather belt. The advice may be financial: a classic cashmere coat is an investment buy that will never date. And the advice is also practical. Jess Cartner-Morley in the *Observer* reminds us that "the greatest advantage of moving your waistline higher is that it eliminates that draught down the back of low-waisted trousers or jeans while sitting down".

It is true that many more pages are addressed to women than are addressed to men. This in turn is because the lifestyle magazines are mainly intended for women. Whether this is because men are more confident of their appearance, or more indifferent to it, or more frightened to think about it than women are, I can hardly say. The man–woman balance of fashion pages suggests perhaps that women are over-anxious about their appearance – a hang-on, possibly, from the days of Veblen and "conspicuous consumption", when the main commission of some women was to work on their appearance – while men are under-anxious, whatever the reason. For it is not that men necessarily look so great, taken at random in the street. And the fashion pages that are devoted to men suggest that a number of them share the concerns of young women. So a young man may be offered a yellow cardigan, £20, by Red Herring at Debenhams, trousers, £10, by George of Asda. The model who wears these particular items stands with a diffidence, and frowns as though he were not completely keen to be photographed. In this he differs from the girl models, who, quite often, meet our eyes, and slightly purse their lips.

Fashion news reports on a busily productive industry, and clearly helps sales. But it also seems to feed an urgent appetite: a voracious desire to absorb new clothes, both by shopping and also vicariously, with the eye. It is as if, no matter how many clothes we had or saw, they never could be enough, or as if we had a form of nakedness that actually was hard to clothe. There are several kinds of worry that our clothes may help us to meet, and it may be that the anxiety of the naked body is not the most important. For it is not merely that naked we come forth into this world – desperate we come forth into this world, and naked of all identity. There is an anxiety at the back of life, and it may be that clothes help us to meet it. Anxiety ensures that, for all our lives, we compete. Anxiety may wake us at three in the morning, for anxiety is the wound that will not heal: religion and politics play to it. But it is better to be covered at three in the morning, than naked. Covers of any sort mitigate this vulnerability, and familiar clothes are friends: their soft touch on our skin has a kindly reassurance, as we find out in dreams, when our clothes cheat on us and disappear, and we are helpless as babes in ancient fearfulness. Perhaps for all of our lives clothes are, to a small extent, strips of blanket, walking wombs, crawling cauls.

For this form of comfort probably any clothes would do. And presumably the best cure for anxiety consists not in clothes at all, but in loving and being loved, and one may also wrap oneself in the lover's love as in the most sumptuous fur. But it also helps our anxiety if we are reminded that we are somebody, for the primal fear is that we are nobody. And clothes give us standing. Stylish clothes show that we are not a football, at the mercy of any event: they say top-drawer, success, on trend. Cutting-edge clothes feed the sense of superiority – superiority to most people, who are not with that style – and perhaps nothing goes so far to assuage aboriginal worry as the sense of superiority, whereas anxiety thickens towards depression if we give the impression of being low in the heap. Nineteenth-century cartoons in *Punch* were rather good at bringing home how stoutly secure the smartly dressed felt, and how laughably awkward the unhappy were, in bagged clothes that let them stand all at odds.

Our clothes are not so harshly divisive as were the rich clothes of rank in the old class societies: the societies that Veblen and Simmel described. But anxiety is surely a part of the story if one looks, in the fashion pages, at the whole subject of trends, "trend" being the on-trend name for fashion. For there are two kinds of letter in the fashion correspondence columns. One kind asks, "What should I wear? How *shall* I look good, and still look me?" This is a sympathetic question. But the other kind of letter says, "Tell me – quickly – what is the trend? How may I get on trend at once?" This is where one's anti-fashion itch may flare. Why is it so important to be "on trend"? Why can't people just dress as themselves? That is how the fashionable have always been mocked. So Kant called the fashionable vain and foolish, and Simmel referred to "dependent natures". It is not those who set new fashions who are guyed, but those who follow slavishly, the fashion victims: those who are impatient to be the shadow of someone else, as if their greatest wish was that the celebrity trend-setter, meeting them in the street, should think that he or she was looking in a mirror – until the fashion victim says, with an awkward grimace, "Hi, I'm me – isn't it great to look like you?"

Who would want to stand in that relation to someone else? Except that those "on trend" will not see it like that. For they surf beside the leader on the crest of the human wave, leaving Mr and Mrs Average splashing all at sea behind them. There must be an exhila-ration too in running with the herd, as against grazing among the ruminants. As every car ad reminds us, we get a lift from movement regardless of direction or destination. And the essence of fashion is movement, and change in changing directions. To be moving fast with the best and not left behind must be another answer to the insecurity of existence, especially in a society as atomized, as over-crowded, and in an odd sense as *equal,* as our own society, where it is so easy to be lost to sight in the mass.

Nor should I make the on-trend items seem more outlandish than they are. A shoe-boot – a "shoot" – is not outrageous. Recent trends have been: bright prints, belted styles, metallics, patents, "masculine tailoring", and the classic military-style coat. Some of these might even seem tame beside the big ruffs, big bustles and codpieces of the past. "Tartans!" exclaims the *Observer* magazine, "a trend for winter and a trend we are liking, surprisingly". *Company* recently told its young readers, "the trend is country checks and tweeds", an announcement that would enable the royal family to wake up and find they had arrived "on trend". It is true that the effect was more aggressive when these two trends were joined in one. As *New Woman* put it, "get punk'd this autumn/winter with tough tartans and cool checks", or again, with a somewhat British National Party inflection, "tough tartans and cool checks means Britannia rules, OK!" Other street trends are far from street-aggressive. For the trend may be for chunky knitwear: not any chunky cardie, but a cloud-shaped knitted short-coat, worn with straight-leg jeans.

If, that is, one has the figure of a fashion-model, and is shaped like a wisp of wire. Otherwise, stay off the trend, the fashion aunts advise. Their tone is wry, for they know their divided responsibility, which actually they discharge with a great deal of tact. They announce the trends, which their readers are hungry to know, but also they must help their readers look good, which some trends hardly will. Tactfully they advise the tall to buy a princess-style coat on the large size, so it will not look tight. Designers, visiting their pages, concur. "Dress for yourself," Savannah Miller advises, "rather than religiously following trends". She loves, she says, "the androgynous trend", but treats it as a fun thing. The cropped tuxedo jacket looks good, but neither she nor the readers of the fashion pages should be caught being trend-victims.

To an extent, it may be that the fashion journalists make up the trends for readers who are anxious that there *should* be trends. Also, the journalists help us with the other monster-movement, the brand. For they must choose between brand and brand, and cannot afford to be label victims. Actually they are quick to say if – because of deaths and successions at the top – Versace, say, loses its way then finds it again. Thus readers find currents that they can join, so they can be select without being alone. Fashion aims for a measured conspicuousness in order to hold opposing anxieties at bay: the anxiety of being lost in the old drab crowd, and the anxiety of being a lonely style freak. But whatever one says in guying brands and trends – or in noting the worries that give them power – actually modern society looks a good deal less like a fashion victim than societies used to look in the past. Then, among the fashionable, the top hats on gentlemen's heads slowly extended then slowly subsided, pretty much in unison, like telescopic chimneys. In unison the crinolines gathered backwards into bustles, and gradually rose, then gradually sank, like the slow flanks of a sleeping hippopotamus (the hippopotamus being society). The relation in which people stand to trends is more individual now, especially since at any time there are many trends to choose from, the more so since the fashion year now has many more seasons than four (there is summer, then the holiday season, which is different, then autumn, then winter (1), then Christmas, then the Sales, then winter (2) ...). Also those who are on trend will wear the trend with a difference, with a personal "accent", an individuating touch – and sometimes with so many accents and touches that the trend is hardly seen, feebly waving as it drowns. So people show they are alert to life, and know where it's going, while with a scarf or a bag, with eye-liner or a tie, they mark their independence.

As to the trends – the fashions – themselves, it is easy to mock the merry-go-round vacuity of it all. This autumn's colour is purple, then black is back, then grey is the new black, then blue is black, then black is back (again). The waist is down, then the waist is up – and higher up – is that to allow for obesity, however thin the models may be? Maybe not, the waist is plunging down again, towards the knees. It all seems like change for change's sake, with a good deal that is ridiculous about it. Veblen himself argued that fashions changed so rapidly both so that the wealthy could waste more money faster – for all to see – but also because fashions had become so ludicrous that even the wealthy could not bear them for long. But Veblen was a hard-bitten satirist as much as a level analyst. Many fashions did and do look good: and if fashions change, well change is life, and innovation is new life. We shouldn't complain if fashions are changeable when in the arts we have an appetite for new talents and new thoughts. And if the whole world of fashion has its folly and vanity, as so many commentators have said, still some fashions have had a point to make.

For although trends and fashions veer and change constantly, fashion is not purposeless. Through the changing "seasons" there will be a slow movement in a certain direction, which suits the way in which the economy and the habits of life are changing. The large slow changes would perhaps occur anyway, but undoubtedly they are helped in their progress by stylish individuals with sensitive antennae, who in some sense see the future. The "merry monarch" Charles II had this gift. Merry as he was, and although brought up in France, he reacted against the colours and the ribbons of Versailles. He thought men's dress should be more simple, sober and dark. Being king, he believed he could lead this change, and actually he did so. He appeared in court in a long dark coat with buttons from top to bottom, and the courtiers who smirked to see him look so strange soon found it wise to "follow suit", for he had just invented the suit.

King Charles was not alone in this invention: the king of Sweden was to have similar plans, and in France too men's styles were growing plainer. But still Charles was a kind of dress pioneer. It is true that in the seventeenth and eighteenth centuries the suit was loose and elaborate by our idea of tailoring. But then in England's Regency, more than a hundred years after King Charles, George

"Beau" Brummell launched what was called the "dandy" style. It differed from earlier fopperies by being extremely simple, and tightly cut, tending to dark tones and black. Brummell sought to avoid display, saying, "If John Bull turns to look at you in the street, you are not properly dressed". He himself cut a dash, at assemblies and the gaming tables, but what essentially he had done was to provide the prototype for the plain, smart, dark outfit that all Victorian England was presently to wear, with a still more sober and sombre demeanour. Much of his style is with us still, in dark-toned power suits worn both in the City and in society.

Brummell was not alone in his fashion, any more than King Charles had been: there were other dark dandies, and there was a broader trend, for men, towards sombre tailoring. But still, in the weird world of fashion, King Charles and Beau Brummell were a form of avant-garde: they were kinds of prophet, like Moses dressed in Jacob's coat (or rather, in a smart dark coat) leading the people to the promised wardrobe. And the fashionables who followed them, all vain at being "on trend", were at least walking towards the future, not into a retro cul-de-sac.

In women's clothes there is Gabrielle "Coco" Chanel, who in the 1910s and 1920s, in a world of embroidered, beaded, flower-patterned dresses, draped on her models simple black modernist rectangles of cloth. One rectangle made a little black dress, two rectangles made a woman's smart suit – so the pattern was set for women's sharp suits, in the professions and at leisure, through the twentieth century. Chanel, again, was not alone, there were other women designers moving in the plain direction: but it was Chanel who had the obsession, the decision, to crystallize the way that fashion should go.

To say that trendsetters have seen the future is not to say that they were nice to know. It does appear that King Charles was merry, and he was the king. But Beau Brummell was a frigid snob, and Coco Chanel got by well enough when the Nazis were in Paris.

Both Brummell and Chanel lived alone and died alone, and had something of the austere solitary about them in the centre of the social throng. One could say they paid a human price for investing their vitality in the masquerade of clothes: and perhaps no break-through is made without sacrifice. A less well-known pioneer was Rita Lygid. She was not a designer, but she did cause a sensation in the 1920s by being the first woman to wear in society a dress – of her own design – that was bare at the back to the waist. She was the Liz Hurley of her day, although at the back not at the front. She was however more successful than Liz Hurley as a fashion leader. The sensation that she caused was at first a scandal, and she was excori-ated: but presently other bare backs of ladies appeared, and soon it was clear that the scandal had mutated into a fashion.

As with Brummell and Chanel, there was something tragic about Lygid. Her marriages broke and the love of her life, with a New York Episcopalian minister, failed. Like Brummell she bankrupted herself through extravagance, spending too much on clothes and buying vast gossamer wheels of crochet-work to decorate her apartment. Like Brummell again, she died alone in poverty and pain. Yet each contemporary party dress that neatly turns to show that it has no back is a small, unknowing memorial to her.

Perhaps her invention would not have become the fashion, if she had not been attractive, and rich, and a patron of the arts – or if she had lost confidence at the crucial moment, and had slunk from the opera house, her back aflame with shame. One might say that uncovering their back was not a terribly important thing for anyone to do, and that it is odd of me to imply that her act was a statement or some sort of art-event. And yet her dress, her uncov-ered back, marked a stage in another gradual change of fashion: the momentous and extraordinarily slow striptease that women have practised for the past five hundred years, uncovering at the rate of twelve inches to the century their forearms, their upper arms, their shoulders, back and legs.

Striptease is the wrong word, of course, because in women's terribly tardy emergence from the chrysalis of their clothes there has been an enfranchisement, rather than just a display. For it is not that women in the West bare their arms, or their legs, all the time. On the contrary, women have also adopted, and adapted, the body-covering styles of men. Women wear trousers and jackets and suits when they want to, moulded so as to fit a woman's body elegantly. Women do not wear clothes less than they did, but they have developed an unprecedented freedom in the relation in which they stand to their clothes. They are released from the obligation to be enclosed in cloth for nearly all of the time. This is not a freedom that men have yet: men may escape from their clothes on the beach and at the pool but otherwise they are pretty much wrapped up.

It seems that when we put on clothes we sheathe ourselves in a social shadow: an ethos, an ethic, that guides and limits. The slowness with which women's styles have found their freedom indicates what hard, slow work it is to come out from under that kind of shadow, which sits upon us in the form of approved or "decent" dress. From this point of view, the changeableness of fashion looks not like fickleness, but like a sign of life: it shows an unwillingness to be kept in a single, standard container. And it may only be when the person container, the clothing, is in a condition of perpetual inconstancy – the condition of fashion – that it is practicable for the large, grand changes to make their way. In the wake of the strutting dandies the look of everyone slowly alters, as if the tectonic plates of general social change were gigantic bolts of cloth.

Where these slow changes have brought us – aided by modern politics and modern economics – is to a world in which both men and women can make more choices as to lifestyle, travel, politics, faith and intimate orientation than has been possible in the past. Perhaps it is too much a free-for-all. Might we get lost among the fashions, and among the different play-selves that trend upon trend has given to us? But this is not what happens, because the overriding injunction is that we all should *be* ourselves. Of course, we may all be so busy doing much the same kind of self-work that we end up having similar sorts of selves. But that is not how it looks. We are visibly disparate, and in our pencil-skirts and full-length skirts and white jeans and wide-leg trousers, in our tabards and tops and puffball shirts, in our jumpsuits and plain suits and ties and T-shirts and baggy zip-up tops we *look* more diverse than human societies used to do. In Jane Austen's time, ladies in general wore empire-line gowns: very many of them could have been Jane Austen, as nearly all of them were her readers. People do still dress in the large group styles of genders, age groups and income brackets, but also people dress less like each other than they used to in the past. This is partly because of mass production: it is not merely that clothes are mass produced, but also styles – *different* styles – are produced in the mass, so that everyone has so many garments to choose from that it is no surprise if each person has put together their own outfit.

It is naturally so, since individuality is at a premium now. Our clothes say this in so many words, and in actual words too. For we also wear words, more than words were ever worn before. Coats, shirts and trousers have the designer's name on the outside. T-shirts, especially, say a thousand things, and in large-point type, for one seldom reads the same words on any two T-shirts. A facetious T-shirt says "Cannibal Corpse" or "La Puta Madre". A straight T-shirt says "Yellowstone National Nature Park". Other T-shirts joke, and say "Armani Denim Division" when they are certainly not denim and probably not Armani. And for every T-shirt with words printed on it in the factory there is another with a customer chosen message, such as, these are the names of my best friends. And if one asks what the T-shirts are saying in what they say – since they do not often speak philosophy – it surely mainly is: I am different; I am just a fun phrase, but you won't read me on anyone else today; I am an individual, but cool – not a nobody lost in the crowd. The

T-shirts by Katherine Hamnett say more than that, of course: "Save the Rainforest", "Make Trouble", "Free Burma".

It is a question of freedom – the freedom to be oneself, and the freedom to be a freer self than it used to be possible for selves to be. This again is what strikes one, if one flicks through any collection of miscellaneous fashion photos: the range of possibilities, the diversity of the differences. This is especially so in women's fashions, which are so much freer and wilder than men's. I see, for instance: Twiggy in a tight short mini-top with tight short mini-skirt; a girl in sequinned trousers and less than minimal top with her arms stretched upwards outwards to make a far-flung "Y"; two girls in symmetrical punk jersey dresses, one black with shocking pink trim, the other shocking pink with jet-black trim, both with designer rips and tears; a blond model stretching horizontally, drowsily, in a voluminous Bill Gibbs dress that is mounded around her like a tumbled curtain, hugely embroidered and dense with stitched flowers. Newness, difference, individuality, seem together to be the super-trends.

Endless choice, however, does not make life easier. It occurs to me that having sung the varieties of choice, I ought to row back somewhat. For in a world in which the choices are so wide, we could look more different than we do. At times one may feel that there are such diverse styles in play that being in a shopping centre is like visiting the metropolis of an alien galaxy. But, to a longer look, the differences between the outfits are often not so great. There are, for instance, so very many black floppy tops. They may have white or mauve flashes in unique positions, but none of these positions are far apart. Also there are so many blue jeans, a blue ocean of denim. Blue jeans are a sort of classic now – even a new, informal form of uniform – but many of the clothes worn around the shopping centre and are neither classics, nor very different from each other, and if many are brilliant many others are drab.

Drab is popular, one has to admit. In most ages most people seem to have been drab: for drab is good cover, and in a way drab has been the most successful fashion. But what drab means in a world of distinct individuals is that there has been a shared failure of nerve. Nor is it so easy to be an individual. One is so swayed by what other people do, and by the thoughts and words that come out of their mouths and may, before one knows it, come out of one's own mouth too. One has to give oneself a hard time, and read books, and disagree with people, if one is to discover that one has a self that is distinct. Finding the right words for what one wants to say can be difficult, especially if one wants them to be one's own words. In the same way, finding the right clothes can be difficult.

This perhaps is the nub of the question of clothes. However large or small the choice of clothes may be, still the task of finding clothes that are exactly right is demanding and taxing. The reason is that clothes are so intimately connected with us. Finding just the right ones must touch our integrity, and all the difficulties of facing oneself and the world. And if we feel that vanity is also in it, when we stand tall in front of full-length mirrors, still it does not seem entirely an issue of vanity when we seek to help our partner find the right clothes for an important event. As one goes from shop to shop, and from boutique to boutique, issues grow finer and also more fraught because to find the right fit for a quantity as subtle, and delicate, and manifold, as an individual human being is not likely to be easy. For clothes show whether we have depth, or are just a chiffon scarf. Not that finding the right clothes is always hard. We may pick the right outfit at once, and know at once that it is in all ways right. But that, when it happens, has an air of grace about it, as though the universe broke its rules, to let life work perfectly quickly.

This is perhaps the intimate answer to the argument that clothes are merely external, or merely some vain trend or fashion, or a tissue of deceptions that we wish to weave. They have a shadow of seriousness even when they are gossamer light. This returns us to the question of who we are, and who – with the aid of clothes – we may be.

3. What shall I wear, who shall I be?

It is a moot point, of course, how much clothes help us to "be ourselves", and how much they help us to be someone else, such as a role model, or someone we would dearly like to be mistaken for. Nor do we want, necessarily, to expose our private self to the public gaze. People think you naive if you wear your heart on your sleeve. The heart is best kept discreet in its fortified nest behind bones and lungs. We may even, all of us, associate the idea of our true identity with secrets we shall always keep, and certainly not weave into our clothing.

But with all this said, we do use clothes to bring out different "sides": our serious side, or our fun or sexy or reckless side, or our masculine or our feminine side. We may do this deliberately, or quite unconsciously, but when we use our clothes in this way we are bringing something that is inside us outside, perhaps magnifying and enhancing it in the process, and changing the balance of just what we are. We may also change our ethical balance. My granddaughter likes very much a pair of bright red silk pyjamas she has, and says, "I feel very not naughty in these clothes"; my daughter encourages her to keep them on. In other clothes, women may say, they feel wicked and a devil. Men don't say that, I think, but that is part of the way men are closely wrapped up, rather than because they are not wicked or devils.

As to children – or grandchildren – we are likely to clothe them in the way we want them to go. Perhaps we don't do it as simply as people did in the past. Then with clothes you brought out the little sailor in a boy and the little lady in a girl. Now we give in and let them be Spiderman, or a little pony princess in pink. These are subtle moves, however, for Spiderman and Princess Ariel (the little mermaid as was) sweeten the pill of civic virtue. They are enemies of evil-doers and therefore of evil. Or we dress children in denim dungarees, so boys and girls both are like small Bob the Builders. So their clothes say "constructive", even as they pedal full pelt into a sibling's tower of bricks.

In other words, we "put on" virtue with the aim of bringing out the virtue latent within us. In the past stiff starched garments put backbone into people, tight uniforms put discipline into the soldier. Sometimes clothes may work like the exoskeletons of jelly-like creatures which have no bones inside them. There is a wonderful photo by Diane Arbus in which the straw hat, bow tie and chauvinistic badge clearly provide a support system for a young person who looks worryingly fragile.

In these cases the movement is from outside to inside: the clothes have designs on the person within them – they will melt if they can through his skin into his bones. It may also be that clothes can make feelings deeper. It may be that in the past, mourning dress, when they had to wear it, helped the bereaved to give themselves more wholly to grieving. (It is true that mourning clothes may also have worked, like some expressions of face, as a substitute for feeling – your clothes, and sad look, could do the mourning for you.) Special clothes at a wedding, or a shining white dress, may give an extra and special lift to a rather delicate pitch of happiness. Keeping the dress afterwards, even wrapped in polythene at the back of the attic, may be a kind of remembering, so a certain emotional pitch is kept alive, although in reserve, with a sort of private piety. In a case like this, clothes may help us to possess our soul, and we may place our soul within the clothes.

Clothes are like a lens: they bring us, or a part of us, into focus, and push the less wanted selves back towards the shadows. Some clothes will give us an inner ease, and help us to be elegant, even debonair, while our worries are pushed off with our workaday clothes. Or smart clothes, for an interview, will help us get our mental act together. We like our clothes to match our mood, even to intensify the mood of the moment. So party clothes can be freedom, expectation in the shape of loose unbuttoned sleeves, exhilaration in the lift of chiffon panels: the fluttering looseness can reflect, can be, a flickering impatience to dance. For the movement may also be from inner to outer. And whatever I have said of the darker secrets, even secrets may creep towards the surface, and seek at once half to show and half to hide themselves. They may thread themselves through the cloth of a sleeve, even if they are not worn proud on the sleeve. So in Marcel Proust's *À La Recherche du temps perdu*, Baron de Charlus betrays discreetly his forbidden sexuality in the red thread that runs, just discernibly, through the weave of his tweeds.

Or again there is underwear, intermediate clothing: worn above our skin, yet hidden as our skin is hidden. Some of our secret self may hover – a delicacy, a daringness – in that ambiguous zone, recognized by us, yet incognito. It was perhaps so with Henry James. When a friend visited James unexpectedly on a torrid summer's day – away from London, in his lovely old house at Rye – he found the elderly author sitting in his garden finishing an article, wearing nothing but red underpants. Probably they were the line in gentleman's red underpants that were sold in the 1900s by Jaeger. It may be they meant nothing, but equally it may be that for James they represented – beneath the dark pinstriped trousers and the carefully brushed coat of his sedate and sedulous daily persona – a hidden vein of zest or passion.

Putting the underwear back into its drawer, we may feel that our different outer garments show not so much different sides to us as different layers. Our work clothes may be the external layer, our public persona for work in the world, while the slops we put on when we get home are like pyjamas: they *are* our rest and relaxation. Our muscles ease, we de-stress as we put them on, but they are inner clothes, not for public sight; we would change even if a friend came round.

To take an extreme, a man may wear one kind of clothes in the office, even uptight clothes, a white shirt, an institutional tie, a dark blue jacket like a blazer, all suitable to his short-back-and-sides haircut. Then at night he may be glimpsed in the badlands the other side of town, flitting through under-lit streets in stylish black leather from head to foot, including a black leather cap. That man has two personae, then – two acts, two performances, perhaps one should say – but both are him, and I find myself thinking then that the night-man is hidden *inside* the day-man, perhaps as Superman, in skin-tight blue with Jaeger-red briefs, is hidden within the suit, Clark Kent. One could, I suppose, equally say that even when on the hunt, at night, blazer-man hides inside black-leather-man. But that feels wrong. I think of blazer-man at night as a discarded carapace, rather as Clark Kent's suit must lie all crumpled inside the phone booth, until Superman swoops back and slips it on again. Blazer-man seems outer, because he is more public, available by daylight to be seen by anyone, whereas leather-man seems inner both because he is more covert, coming out by night, and also because he looks like desire on the loose. In any event, the two outfits seem not so much to reflect as almost to *be* two selves. In summer, it may be, the truly inner man may also be seen, stretched out at a resort and systematically tanning a well-worked-out body. But that motionless, tautly biding body may too seem then like an outer garment, deep within which a keen figure in black stalks onwards through the excited night.

This talk of selves is a kind of shorthand, and if we have more than a single self, we certainly have more than two stark selves. Life is more complicated than a day–night, dark–light divide. The term "personae" may be more useful than "selves", since the "persona" was originally the mask that the actor held in front of his face to identify the character he was performing: the old man, the hero, the proud soldier, the clown.

If I turn the camera towards myself, and think of the different personae that other people see in me, then I realize that, however much one may believe one dresses for onself, one does also dress quite a lot for other people. The sense of an audience is important for clothes, and there always is an audience. Even when one is alone, one is aware how one *would* look to someone one cared for. In the changing cubicle in the shop or the discount outlet, trying on clothes with concern, I am not alone with the garments. This is not only because I like my wife to come with me when I shop because I depend hugely on her initiatives, steers and comments. In any case, I am choosing my clothes a good deal with a view as to how they will strike other people.

I dress for my students, for instance, probably more than they or I think that I do. It seems stuffy to wear a jacket and tie these days, but when I give a lecture I always wear some sort of jacket: often a leather jacket, because leather jackets seem less staid than woollen jackets. This must be for protection, because there may be many eyes on me – as one protects one's vulnerable lower body by standing behind a lectern. And as to jackets, it is true that I like the leather jacket. I like its supple looseness, and the way it is bigger and broader than I am, and lets me shift and sidle inside it. I can see that it is part of an outer persona, and that it does some work for me while I can relax. A shirt is more personal because it is an inner garment. One needs I think to like one's shirt, and by chance as I write this I am wearing a shirt that I do like a lot: a plain grey cotton shirt with a slightly canvas-like durable feel to it. When I wear it I feel I am close to a good thing; I do wear it more for myself than for other people.

There is a reciprocity in one's relations with one's clothes, an intimacy in the connection between two different kinds of entity, the garment and the person. With a tie, when one wears a tie, the relationship is more demonstrative. For a tie sends signals to the outer world, even as it winds inside collars and coats. So I find it a cop-out when a tie only speaks of clubs and colleges, professions and income-brackets: then a tie seems like a boring remark. And I am enough of a connoisseur to watch Channel 4 News not only because I like its politics, but in order to see which tie Jon Snow will wear today. No other anchorman compares with him for a *good* originality of design and colour.

Ties are like tiny catwalk shows, as if all that women's clothes may display – in bright colours and daring colours, and startling curving lines and shapes – may be performed for men in the tiny lozenge, or vertical strip, that hangs down from their necks. Of course, that display may be grossly done, in ties that should be torched on sight. But good ties are something: clearly they are the part of menswear that can show men in touch with their feminine side, as women's clothes, nowadays, have many touches of the masculine. In my case this is no surprise, since the ties I like the best have been given to me by my wife and daughter. For although clothes may reflect our selves, they are also a collaborative venture. We wear them for other eyes, and probably we have chosen them with the help of others. Perhaps the truly best clothes both exist for, and are the product of, good relations with other people.

I am divided about ties, however, because another part of me dislikes constraint at the neck; and I am similarly divided, I suppose, about suits although, not being in business, I don't often need to wear one. But I can see that in a formal or public encounter one needs the reinforcement of some kind of shield, and a suit is a good shield. I can see too that a more expensive suit may make a better shield. We rely a good deal on the support of clothes when we need to give any kind of performance. We are not likely, most of us, to perform on the stage, but there are many kinds of performance in life, at big or small meetings, at parties or in the pub, in the family or

perhaps in court. Then the suit-of-rare-occasions is a valuable auxil-
iary, whether one is explaining a deficit to shareholders, or saying
what one must as best man at a wedding. The suit-of-rare-occasions
is like a stronger, better body: as it were, one's best body, because it is
part of one's *best* self, which one needs to be to face the challenge.

Perhaps I exaggerate, speaking now of man the actor, of man or
woman as a theatrical animal. But – to put myself for the present
on the back-burner – we learn early on that life is a performing
art. Children tell stories before they know too well the difference
between lying and telling the truth. Very early they learn to mime
feelings – misery, excitement – that will steer adults in the way
they desire. Animals too perform, to entice a partner or scare off
rivals and assailants. Birds display and sing to attract a mate, and
one might then think that the human race displays and sings not on
a seasonal basis, but at all times, as though it wished to mate with
everyone. For everyone likes to be liked, and maybe the primary
human performance is to *please*: to please, so that one is liked. It
may be only when one is secure in feeling liked by the person who
matters – a parent, a partner, a peer group – that one lets other
motives kick in, like showing off aggressively and wanting to make
other people jealous. Clothes are accessories in all these performances. Perhaps one reason why we dress so as to look quite a lot
like other people is so that they will like us as they like themselves.
Nice-looking clothes are an offer of friendship. In addition they
are a cover we can hide behind if all fails and we are not liked. The
confidence in their smartness will continue to assert for us, even if,
within, we are getting more nervous.

Women's clothes do these things more openly: more vulnerably,
perhaps more anxiously, and certainly more beautifully. But the
man's smart suit is a guarded way of doing the same thing. Suits
have had a bad press in recent decades, since supposedly dull executive types came to be called "suits" in the 1970s. More recently
still there has been a turn, however; witness the current acclaim,

in the fashion theory press, for Cary Grant. Cary Grant was the son of an English tailor's cutter and throughout his later career in Hollywood he supervised with loving care the suits he wore in films and elsewhere. He had eight identical suits made to play the single suit that he wears through *North by Northwest*. He is always elegant, even when he dives through dense corn while sprinting from a murderous crop-duster plane. He and his suit together are manly, kindly and likeable: they put us at our ease because they are at their ease, as if life were a cocktail party where one never got drunk, and where everything said was just a little ironic without showing malice or side.

It was not for nothing, though, that suits did pass through a trough of mistrust. A suit may be a formidable prop in a performance, and some suits are definitely not to be trusted. Like for instance the aluminium-ish suits that young salesmen may wear, suits that are part of the sales pitch and help the young salesman to be radically unreliable. Again, a dark suit underlined the grave tones of Tony Blair when he assured us that there were weapons of mass destruction in Iraq. For a suit does not exaggerate; it claims restraint and responsibility. I suppose that the suits that are worn by newsreaders say "Trust me, these *are* the facts", as a coloured shirt would not. It is because he wears a trustworthy suit that Jon Snow can show a tasteful flamboyance in ties.

There also are power suits, which warn you that it is in your interest to trust them. Discreetly padded and moulded, they sculpt a power body, strong in the shoulder and mobile at the waist: both the suit, and the implied body, speak determination. They say: you can trust me to run the firm or the nation, because you see I can run my body – govern it and keep it fighting fit. Power suits are sheathes, with the purpose of making the wearer resemble a sword. They offer, if they work, efficiency, success, money.

If they work ... For I realize that in all that I've said, I've assumed the cooperation of person and garment. But life is not so tidy. We may not find the right clothes, or not do the right thing with them. For clothes can also give you away: they can give away your income, a vulgarity, a failure of cool. And maybe, since we are vigilant social animals, we are on the lookout for the give-away side of clothes. Those lectures that I give are often about novelists: actually, novelists are a disappointment to dress historians, because normally they will not say what the hero or the heroine wears. But novelists are quick to catch disparities. Charles Dickens says of the unhappy schoolmaster in *Our Mutual Friend*, "he was never seen in any other dress, and yet there was a certain stiffness in his way of wearing this, as if there were a want of adaptation between him and it". And Anne Enright says of a character in *The Gathering*, "his clothes seemed to mock his body". The fashion aunts in the magazines, and those who write in to them, know how easy it is to wear the wrong clothes. Chunky knitwear may be on trend, but you had better not wear it if you are chunky already. Slanting lines will help you seem curvaceous if you are lean and straight, but they will do you harm if you have a figure that Rubens would have loved. And these are the simplest cases, getting clothes to help the body shape. There are many ways in which clothes betray people, even smart clothes. In Tolstoy's *Anna Karenina*, the city dandy Vasenka Veslovsky knows he made a gaff when he joins a hunting party in a new hunting outfit and sees that the rest of the gentry have come in their *old* country clothes.

What is so treacherous about clothes is that everyone else may know, and you may not, if they are letting you down. Because, if you did know, you would not have worn them: and they are what everyone *sees*. Perhaps this again is why men have worn suits, in their safely limited set of variations. Men have seemed to be more nervous than women of running risks in their clothes. Perhaps it is from modesty, although some might say that men dress more covertly because they are lying in wait, preferring to be the one who desires, rather than the object of desire. Even so they are vulnerable, for you are always a little more on the alert when someone else comes up to you wearing a suit. You wonder, has he something to sell? Does he want to enlist you in a new religion?

All of which, to relax at last, is why one does not wear a suit when eating either out or at home with friends; to wear one would mean that they were not friends. I left out friends when I was talking of audiences. But it may be that one most likes to put on "best clothes" (suits apart) when one is going out with friends. If so, one is dressing for them *out of* friendship: it is one way of showing that one likes to be with them.

But I am forgetting my age. For the kind of best clothes that my wife and I wear to see friends would probably rate the same on the smartness index as the clothes that we used to wear long ago, when we went, singly, to a party, with the thought that we might find a partner. Dressing up to have dinner with friends allows one to recapture a little the zest of young parties, but innocently, without the targeting of the mating game, and without the hazard and worry of it. I guess the same might be said when one dresses to go to a private view, or to the theatre, or to some other of culture's display arenas.

For the sort of smart dressing one does with friends – what may now be called smart-casual, since it has no serious end in view – is a distinctly relaxed version of what was the real thing. The true real thing is the dead-serious dressing to attract – so as to couple or to mate – that causes young people to try on twenty best outfits in anguish, preparing for the key encounter. This is where clothes matter most of all, and where their "protective function" is least an issue: in the wild hunt, the partner-chase. There display is vital; it goes with the tracking and scenting and snatching, the rage of attraction, the despair of rejection. There the different, stunning look is everything: it is life and success or one might as well kill oneself.

I must forget myself and what I wear: youth is at the centre of the life of clothes. At night outside clubs I may weave my way through them, past whitened faces, hair that is jet-blacked or gelled in short spines, past men in T-shirts and girls in next to nothing who bawl their laughter in the freezing gale – exposing arms and bust, midriff and thigh – with extraordinary audacities, or vulgarities, of colour. I notice them but they do not see me, for I am invisible because I am older. If, back in my study, I turn to journals of fashion theory, there again the analysis is of youth subcultures, and the complications of retro chic: the Pop Art look, the Op Art look, and the gaffes the unwary make when they put on a mid-1960s mini-dress (a replica, in which the armholes do not have the authentic 1960s' tightness) together with platforms that are clearly *late*-1960s. And if I turn to the weekly and weekend fashion supplements, yet again it is a world of teen or twenty-somethings. The models are attractive and young, and the designer names are youthfully shaved to a single syllable: taupe belt by Cos, sheer tights by Cette, Fred at Tesco. If the names are longer, they are funny, like Mango or Nougat: it is true that the odd ancient name survives of a line that has managed to be at once venerable and cutting-edge, such as Balenciaga. There are scoop necks and cowl necks, V-necks and button-necks, and halter necks and funnel necks – and still even polo necks – but all of them are young necks. There are styles again that look best on the young – cable knit and chunky knit, the jacquard dress and pinafore dress – and nearly all of them in the supplements are well designed. Truly we live in a paradise of clothes, and even if many of them end up in landfill sites, still the production of more of them races, and is endless. For the fast money is "young money", to an extent not seen before in history. Here at the youth end is the crucible, the ferment, the volcano of dress invention and dress production, flaring in the furnace of closely packed young people jumping on the spot better to look out for partners. Here trends change rapidly, skirts soar and plunge, sleeves lengthen and shorten and loosen and tauten, and colours change like a firework display. For all the fairground flurry and fashion bazaar, the conspicuous instant consumption of fat young pay-packets in a conflagration of fabrics, are not there for their own sake. They have a further purpose. The writhing, shimmering, yawning clothes find endless ways of hinting or showing the desirable young body within the clothes. They show it in glimpses, a magic creature of attraction, for the whole swirling Salome's dance of uncoverings is concerned with the human spindle within them. Clothes cosset it and clasp it and conceal and reveal it, and make it seem to be in change for ever, because the play of dress is a play of dress-dreams and dream-bodies until the moment when consummation comes, and with a languorous sigh or with stumbling impatience the clothes slip off or rip off, they unzip and divide and disappear, and body joins body with no envelope intervening.

Still, the youth end cannot be the whole story. Looking back at the older folks – those who make the most conspicuous show of their clothes – we may wonder quite what game it is that the famous dandies are playing. The Beau Brummells, the Counts d'Orsay: they sport clothes that seem made for the mating game with little purpose of mating, but simply to be adored for a *perfect* display. There seems an odd short-circuiting here, an arrest at the exorbitant-ego stage of the young peacock's life, protected as he advances into adulthood by a sort of inner ice. Then, it may be, Narcissus can give fashion leadership, although fashion leadership is the ghost form of leadership: it may guess the future, but it has no power.

For power is the other issue to which clothes relate: love at the youth end, without substantial social power; and power at the older end – success, position – perhaps without much love. Clothes matter most vitally and importantly to us, and we choose our clothes with the greatest urgency, in those places and times when it is we who are most anxious to be chosen. Behind our choices is the terror that we may not be chosen. There are different rules of course for those who want to be chosen as partners, and those who would be chosen to lead: the politicians, the would-be chief executives, the promotees in every firm and team. Being chosen for leader does not require that clothes uncover skin, nor that the body be made beautiful by teasing; the work of power clothes is to simulate power without causing fear. But still power clothes speak body non stop: the power suit, both for men and for women, models a figure that is shapely in addition to seeming strong. For power clothes like partner clothes need to seduce: to seduce as well as to impress. So power clothes to some extent resemble love clothes, for the competitors will succeed better if they are also sexy, and can win desire as well as regard. And love clothes, for their part, will resemble power clothes. Because would-be partners also need to show competitive strength: love me, love clothes say but, to rivals, back off. So power clothes clothe and reveal the will, as love clothes show will and desire together. Power clothes sheathe the tiger, as love clothes reveal, at a hundred points, Eros.

For most of our life, nonetheless, we are not at the crisis point of being either chosen or chucked. Our clothes, and choosing them, are a part of life. If we get them right, it will be with help of many kinds from others. And getting clothes "right" means what? There is no absolute value or good in clothes. If we ever were the last man or woman left in the world, our clothes would have no meaning at all. They might keep us warm, but who would want to live, then? But they would not be in any sense right, because what makes clothes right is a matter of meeting happily, and in a way that has something fresh about it, a diverse bunch of expectations that are shared with other people. Not that anything can ever please everyone, nor can one be trying to please all day long. Perhaps in the end it is simplest to try to please oneself and one's dearest: that is something one can seek to do with integrity, and let the dashing trendy world look after itself.

4. Clothes and the body within the clothes

When Socrates spoke of clothes, he made clear his preference to do without them. And about the exposed body, philosophy may be eloquent. Wittgenstein said, rather wonderfully, "the human body is the best image we have of the human soul". Moral commentators – within Christendom – have placed a different stress. The human body may be in the image of God, but it is also fallen, unruly, an oven of sin: just the sight of it is dangerous, an incitement to lust. Through the mid-seventeenth century – the "puritan" period – a succession of public moralists, such as Thomas Tuke and Joseph Hall, denounced revealing dress. They complained of dresses that bared women's arms "beyond that which is fit for every one to behold", and that "laid forth to mens view" their breasts. From this point of view clothes are virtuous: they can protect us from temptation as they protect us from the cold. Thus clothes become a moral fence, enclosing our sinfulness and frustrating the desires of others.

The division of views is reflected in Hans Andersen's famous story "The Emperor's New Suit". The story satirizes the vanity of a ruler, and a ruling class, for whom fine clothes are excessively important; also the readiness of people to lie rather than say something that might be thought stupid, even if the lie is utterly preposterous, such as claiming that empty air is a fine-spun suit of cloth-of-gold. Fashion itself is empty, the story seems to imply, and the true fashion in the story is in a sense intellectual, and consists in the demonstration that a ludicrous fiction may become the belief of nearly everyone, except for the child, who sees, and says, that "The Emperor has nothing on at all". The words make it clear that we should imagine the emperor totally naked, and not wearing under-wear as he often does in illustrations.

What is nice about the story is that it does not end with the child's true words, and the derision of the crowd for the abject nakedness of their foolish ruler. In its last two sentences, the story returns to the point of view of the emperor himself. He sees at once that the child is right, and that he has been foolish and fooled, "but he thought to himself, 'Now I must bear up to the end'". His chamberlains have the same thought, and proceed, like him, to "walk with still greater dignity, as if they carried the train which did not exist". They must make the best of their surreal situation, and mime a splendid dressedness that is not there at all. Actually the story ends with a paradoxical but attractive union of nakedness and clothedness.

We are as divided about our bodies, it seems, as we are about our clothes. It may be *because* we are divided about the body that we are divided about what we want clothes to do. We are not hung-up now about extremely modest coverings, and as to those girls who wear next to nothing when going clubbing on a chilly night, we may be more amazed by their hardiness than dismayed by their undress. On the other hand, if one thinks of the plunging Versace dress that Liz Hurley so famously wore at the première of *Four Weddings and a Funeral*, really it uncovered little more than many dresses uncover. The shock was in the absence of any small link or strap of fabric, such as normally would connect the two front halves of a revealing dress. Her dress looked, as a result, as though with the first breeze it could peel right open. It did not peel open, but even cutting-edge types were startled by it: as if a dress could be tantamount to nakedness. The instinct for modest covering hides within us, and would spring into spasmodic life if our partner came to meet us in a cinema foyer wearing only what they wore at the pool in the morning.

We had better not be hard on modesty, prissy as modesty sometimes seems. Even if our own conventions have changed, we probably still respect modesty when we see it operating for Muslim girls. We soon see that they are not in uniform: they don't all wear masks, or vast loose cowls. They have made individual choices as to how they arrange their head-scarves, and their long skirts or loose trousers, because like other people they want to look good while looking themselves. But modesty matters too.

As it matters for us, since we have places where we all wear less – the gym, the changing room, the pool – and places where we all wear more – the office, the superstore, the restaurant. Exposure is much concerned with place, and actually it was always like that. In the past, on a raging summer's day, a whole village would troop off as one to the river, and bathe "in the buff", men and women together. Things became a little different, it is true, in the proper nineteenth century, especially for townspeople. Perhaps I too, since I have said what I wear, should also say what I don't. In the summer in the late afternoon we often go to the same beach in Greece, and are used to bathing and sunning at the naked end of it, with summer friends some of whom we seldom see dressed. And perhaps the proof that in many ways we dress for other people lies in the fact that we also *un*-dress for other people. But that is Greece, and summer holidays, and if we appeared in the same style in the town where we live in England, it would be weird and unthinkable and would probably be perceived as some kind of attack.

There are, it seems, secondary and primary worlds. In some secondary worlds, it is no big deal to be naked: in spare-time, holiday, far-off places. In the primary world of the business of life – the work world of money and serious things – nakedness is unthinkable. Also nakedness in the work world would be erotic, provocative and dangerous, which in the secondary world it is not.

It is almost shocking, in fact, how quickly we recalibrate the erotic register, depending on where we are. If Liz Hurley, in her famous dress, sauntered down a scorching beach, we would think her confused and be sorry to see her so overdressed.

Place is important, so important that in adjusting to different places we come close to acquiring different bodies. The flaccid seaside body abandoned to the sun hardly seems the same as the "smart body" worn with a revealing dress at a distinguished evening party. Also time is important: that is, the century is important. We expose ourselves now to an extent that Western man has not done for millennia, whatever villagers did on hot summer's days. Also gender is important. On the beach now, or in the pool, men and women cover up, or uncover, to pretty much the same degree. At an evening do, on the other hand, the man will cover his legs and his torso and is likely to cover his arms, while his girlfriend's dress is only the more beautiful for being skimpy.

In some places men and women use their clothes in the same way: in other places, they do extremely different things with their clothes. Especially they may differ in how they expose, or conceal, their skin. I have mentioned the extraordinarily slow, historical act of undressing that women have practised through the centuries. In the Middle Ages women were as covered as men, although they sometimes bared their busts in the fourteenth century. Forearms appeared in the seventeenth century, upper arms and shoulders in the nineteenth. From here on matters snowball, or rather the avalanche is of clothes falling off. The back is bared (by Rita Lygid) in the 1920s, together with the lower leg; the leg to upper thigh in the 1960s, and the midriff in the past few years.

None of these stages was for everyone, or for all of the time, and some of them, like bare back and shoulders, were until recently strictly for "smart" formal dos. So what really is remarkable is both the partial nature, and the tardiness, of the uncovering. This process can look like the will to freedom making terribly slow progress against conservative resistance, and that surely is one part of the story. But the other part must be, since the process *was* so slow, that at every stage people in general, including the fashionables, wanted the body to be part-covered as well as being part-exposed. In our own day the area of a woman's body that may almost never be uncovered is very small, although correspondingly important. But we don't see, away from the beach, any massive or overwhelming exposure of body. In daily life the body still needs to be protected. And what happens in the world of fashion is the constant exposing of one body part while covering up another. The locations to be covered, and those to be uncovered, are forever changing places.

There is a taste for both having one's nakedness, and leaving it. This is most obvious in asymmetrical fashions where, with extreme vulgarity in some cases – or with witty sophistication in the dresses of the Japanese designer Yohji Yamamoto – one arm will be covered and the other one shown, or one leg shown and the other covered. Or the bust may be revealed in a plunging *décolletage*, or the back be uncovered precipitously. Or the upper body may wear barely a wisp, while the lower body billows in voluminous silk. Or the upper body may be armoured in folded paper, like an origami style of armadillo, while the legs are exposed in the thinnest of tights.

What is it we like in this fast change of combinations? One could say it is the tease: the constant tease of new glimpses of body. But this seems at best a one-sided answer, because we like the coverings as well as the uncoverings. We show this by using beautiful fabrics for the covering, as if cloth were in a friendly competition with the skin. At the same time we know that if there is a competition, we would prefer for skin to win. Or one could say, it is a question of adornment. We like the bare body, yes, but we also like to "adorn" it, to decorate it, as people do, or used to do, on South Sea islands, where it is so hot all year that clothes are unwelcome. Even so South Sea islanders adorned themselves with beads, tattoos and even garlands of flowers. By doing so, the islanders have said, they saved themselves from being naked. For they too did not want to be wholly naked, any more than we do, even in our central-heated homes.

What one can say is that in the West, for several hundreds of years, both men and women have liked for women, much more than men, to present a body that is part covered and part uncovered. What has changed terribly gradually over history is the ratio of uncovered to covered. There is a long-standing and deep dividedness in us about uncovering the human body: we want to expose it and we want to shield it. Clothes are our soft utensil for managing this division. We do so by keeping one gender mostly covered (men) while inviting the other, women, to be more uncovered. We also do so by inviting women to wear clothes that part cover, and part uncover, the body. Stripteasing, and often changing the locations of exposure, is part of the exhilaration of life: and the basis of excitement is the tension between the desires to cover and to uncover.

Against this one might say that our visual art shows no hesitation about the naked body. From Titian to Jenny Saville, artists have pleased us by showing bare bodies: beautiful female nudes especially, but sometimes elegant Saint Sebastians, punctured with bijoux arrows. It would not be true, however, that there has been no uncertainty, even about the naked Venuses. They have been most acceptable when they have been a little spiritualized, with pensive faces and allegorical meanings. Allegory works like invisible clothing, it seems, making the naked decent. Rubens had difficulty selling the pouchy stripped housewives that he loved to paint to fastidious patrons like Charles I: for Rubens's nudes were not svelte and symbolic-looking in the way that King Charles preferred. On the other hand, it was often not when they were wholly naked, but when they were a trace clad, in a misty loincloth or a "zone", that the nudes in oil-paintings were thought – in their different ways – to be erotic, and dangerous.

In any case the world of painting is another secondary world. Perhaps it is not a holiday world, although the people in paintings seem to lead leisured lives; but still paintings are in another dimension from the primary world of daily business. Ambivalence about the human body, and the sight of it, seems a general fact: it may be expressed in other ways, for instance by lighting. At least, I suppose that people prefer to be intimate by low light or in deep dusk rather than leaving the spotlights on. The body can give rise to many feelings, and can be alarming too: it would be odd if our attitude to it were simple.

But I have myself spoken too simply about covering and uncovering. Since our feelings about the body are divided, clothes themselves may be ambiguous and play double games. Clothes that wrap the body often also find ways to disclose it. Clinging, thin, wet-look dresses reveal the exact form of limb and torso, as tights and stockings do for women's legs, and as men's "hose" did in the Middle Ages. But also full, loose, flowing garments may be of such light material, and gathered so cunningly, that we discern the slender limbs and movements within the rippling envelope. In the past, when women wore bell-shaped skirts, they often also wore a tight bodice, so you saw that the woman had a neat, hour-glass figure. Maybe within the bodice was a corset, but the woman would have worn the corset since adolescence, so that within the corset itself there really was an hour-glass body.

Even with the lower body, the old big skirts would play with the body shape – in odd, caricaturing games, it is true. When women wore hoops to either side of their hips, so they looked wide from in front but shallow from the side, their style played with the fact that women's hips are broader than men's. And when the bustle boomed in the 1870s and 1880s – so women looked deep when seen from the side, although narrow when seen from the front – this style (intriguingly in a moral age) played with the fact that women's bottoms are often plumper than men's.

Men have played other games, which I shall come to presently, games more subtle than the ludicrous codpieces that some men wore for a short stretch of history. But all these dress games with body shapes show that even when clothing covers the body – perhaps especially when it covers the body elaborately – still clothing will "speak" body, and even exaggerate in what it says. There is something light-hearted at the core of this play, a spirit of dress jokes within the dress games, so perhaps we should not ask why fashions change quickly. It would be morose if they did not, if there is wit in them. But there is sensuality also, in the choice of parts to exaggerate. Really what the body exaggerations show is that both men and women can play with style – with the relish of comedy, and without being taken in – the game of make-believing in bodies of delight.

Coverings still cover, and on some occasions still women will clothe the lower body in a long skirt whose shape varies between a cone and a dome. But even here one might say that such conspic-uous protection also draws attention to what is hidden in the cocoon. Perhaps too the emphasis on a neat-figured upper body invites one to guess at a neat lower body beneath the skirt. This is speculative – but while I am being speculative, I shall go on, perhaps irresponsibly, to compare skirt shapes to flower shapes. Samuel Beckett, in his essay *Proust*, says that flowers are shame-less: they disclose their genitals. Women are not shameless: on the contrary, in their modesty, they walk about in skirts that resemble blooms turned face-down to the ground. Both men, and women themselves, as well as much poetry and art, have liked to surround women with bouquets of flowers, and woman may be called by the names of flowers: Rose, Daisy, Lily, Petunia. Women have often liked to embroider flower patterns, and women's clothes are often decorated with flowers. All in all, the woman–flower equation seems well sanctioned, and was so before Picasso painted his girl-friend, Jacqueline, as "La Femme Fleur".

If skirts were shaped like swelling roses and trumpeting lilies – or like tulips, in Christian Dior's "tulip line" of 1953 – still they were modest flowers, directed to the ground. Sometimes these gorgeous blooms have however been lifted high – for instance by the *danseuses* in the Folies Bergères. Then one saw – as we know from the lithographs of Toulouse Lautrec – a froth and foam of petticoats, and within them not the pollen-dusted stamen of a flower but kicking legs, clad in stockings. It remained a thing of knowledge, not sight· the fact that in the centre of all was hidden the actual sex of the woman. For even the *danseuses* were not shameless as flowers, and what they exposed, within their outer layers, were further scalloped and lace-trimmed layers. It may of course be that these inner layers had absorbed the exoticism of sexual contact, at least to the fixed gaze of the delectating gentlemen, sitting forward over their glasses of absinthe, weighing their chances of more private meetings.

A further feature of women's dresses is that nearly all their lines are curved. The old pannier-supported skirts of the eighteenth century and the blooming crinolines of the nineteenth were hugely curved, and hung round with curving festoons and swags. And in the latest issues of *Vogue, Surface* and *Elle*, again I find everywhere big curves swooping and spiralling. Lapels take sensuous ripples, collars yawn gracefully, and shoulder-straps swing in big loops. And this play with curves, which is so inventive and exhilarating in women's fashions, is scarcely to be seen in men's. I am not saying that designer curves invariably echo the curves of women's bodies: sometimes they do, but also they may play fast and loose with women's generous bodily curves. Also the curved outlines, and curved lines of patterns, suggest movement: they are dancing curves, dynamic. Maybe the movement is not even physical, and the curves sway and wheel in a way that reflects the emotional freedom of women. In any event, curves belong especially to women's clothes, and tend to imply a connection on the one hand with the free graph of women's movements in dance and in mood, and on the other with the contour of their bodies, which are more curved than men's.

The models themselves may be more straight-line and angular in their figures. Still, curves play well against straight lines, and the outfits are ultimately meant for women whose bodies may not be so tautly honed. Sometimes you will also see, in the luxurious forward swell of fabric in front of the match-stick figured model, a memory of that non-catwalk condition, pregnancy.

Turning to men, to menswear and to men's bodies, one finds that the changes of history have gone the other way. In the ancient world, where women wore gowns that trailed the ground, warriors – as we know from films like *Gladiator* – wore short skirts. Their arms and legs were bare – and men who were not warriors might wear even less. In Greece they wore the "chiton", a light, short sleeveless tunic. In the Gymnasium philosophers such as Socrates, Plato and their friends worked the punch-ball and wrestled naked, then conversed wisely while naked at the baths. Again in the men's world of the Olympic games, the athletes competed naked. In public older men and orators might declaim enrobed, but the robe consisted of a rectangle of cloth that could be wound round the body before being thrown over the shoulder. The principle of it is simple, but can be elegant. In Greece this garment was called the "hymation", but variations of it have evolved in other countries – most notably in the Roman "toga" – and it is not substantially different from the traditional garment that many women still wear in India.

It is easy to clothe the ancient male if one thinks of many men wearing the toga. But Rome itself was in two minds about the clothing of men. The toga was unpopular with many patricians, who found it cumbersome. The famous Mark Antony went so far in displaying his much-admired physique that he appalled more severe Romans like Cicero. He scandalized many when he publicly urged Julius Caesar to accept the royal crown while he was himself still nearly naked from his involvement in the festival of Lupercalia. Especially he was criticized for going about, from day to day, wearing just a tunic and short cape, and in open sandals. This style caused increasing aggravation to the Emperor Augustus, who issued an edict that all patricians should wear the toga in the forum, that is in public. So if Augustus found Rome brick and left it marble, he also found it free-limbed and left it toga-ed. He was fraily built himself, and in cold weather wore four tunics under his toga. He was much into covering up.

His edict had a poor success, like most attempts to legislate on dress. But in the longer term his wish was fulfilled, and for a good deal longer than the past thousand years men have been so wrapped and swathed and cloaked and clad that you could almost never see more than their faces and their hands. I dare say one should make an exception for Scotsmen, and for men doing manual work in hot weather. Also, in the past fifty years in the West, men have often worn T-shirts and sometimes shorts, and trunks on the beach or in the pool. But still in the primary world of offices, streets, money markets and shops, men have stayed as nervously enclosed as their forebears. And in the recent centuries, in which women have gradually evaded the obligation to be always covered, men have largely preferred to stay under wraps.

It is not that men give no clue to their bodies. On the contrary, men have been as adroit as women at signalling their bodies through their clothes. In the Middle Ages and the Renaissance younger men wore a doublet that was full at the shoulders and tight at the waist, like the caricature of a well-modelled body, while the hose they wore, although never transparent, showed the shape of their legs as distinctly as women's tights do now. Especially, at all times, men have shown off the outline of their thighs, calves and ankles. When breeches became visible below the hem of men's coats, they fitted the thighs closely. And when trousers arrived, they came first as tight-fitting "pantaloons", and later were carefully tailored so that still, within the supple pipe, you saw the athletic calf. Also men used tailoring, assisted by padding and corsets, to model for themselves a dream body that doubtless they hoped would assist their "conquests".

This, moreover, is only part of the story: this pretended transparency, which invites us to trace, within the moulded silhouette, a body worth uncovering. The other thing that men have done – and have done much more than women have – is to remind us of the body in another way: by constantly miming, although seldom completing, the act of starting to take their clothes off. For several hundred years the unfastened fastening has been a feature of menswear: strings, clasps, buckles, buttons, which are often on show but often undone. Coats and jackets have buttons and buttonholes, although often the two sides fail to meet. Many jackets are meant to hang relaxedly open, sometimes over a waistcoat, which will seldom have all its buttons done up.

Men again will seem to want to turn their clothes inside out. Coats and jackets have wide lapels, and used to have big cuffs, which pretend to show the inside of the garment turning outwards. When trousers came in, they in time turned up in turn-ups. Man, as a creature, has a split personality, so he insists on being covered from top to toe, and at the same time implies that he has half a mind to take it all off.

I have spoken about the past, and one might say, "Ah, it's different now". Men go about in T-shirts, and some of them wear shorts in the summer. But if one looks at smart menswear on show in shops, or at those fashion pages that are given over to men, one finds that men's habits have changed very little from how they were a hundred years ago. The suit and tie are still with us. Women gave up any constant commitment to tight neckwear four hundred years ago. It is not that the tight-necked style never returned, and Edwardian ladies were pleased to wear tight-necked blouses. But those ladies too, together with their boned-neck blouses, have passed with the snows of yesteryear, while very many men still tie a soft noose round their necks, as their forefathers fastened tightly their ruffs, bands, stocks and cravats. If the contemporary male model wears a T-shirt, this will come higher up his chest than women's T-shirts ever do. The T-shirt will have short sleeves, but this makes no odds because almost certainly the model's arms will be hidden within a light zip-up jacket.

And still, as in the old days, men will tease their audience by seeming to be about to take their coverings off. The zip, for men, is simply the modern way of playing with openness and closure in the way that men used to do with buttons. Men's zips, in fashion photos, are never done right up (except in one particular place). In the current issue of *Men's Vogue* one model wears a black leather puffer-style jacket with two zips at the front. He has the upper zip pulled down and the lower zip pulled up, so he appears to be peeling open in two directions, perhaps like a banana being opened at both ends. Yet within the upper opening we see a tightly buttoned shirt closely clasped by a tie, which is further gripped by what looks like a large gold safety pin. In other words he is performing his own version of the traditional male non-strip tease.

There are several ways in which men's clothes may seem half ready to come off. One variant is to wear a tie at half-mast, loosely knotted, against a shirt that has the top button open – but only the top button, so little is given away. Another variant is for the tie actually to be undone. In the same issue of *Men's Vogue* another model lets the ends of his bow-tie hang apart, against a shirt that again is only one button open. Where coats and jackets were unbuttoned in the past, so now leather jackets, cardigans and attractive light knitted tops are pretty much unbuttoned or unzipped, while inside all of them is some form of T-shirt, always with the distinctly high male neck. Dillar's, in the same issue, advertise a blue-grey woollen coat which has both buttons and a zip, and the model wears it with both undone. Beneath it is a shirt with two buttons open, and beneath that again the familiar high-necked T-shirt. It seems to be a positive compulsion in men that they should enact aperture on top of aperture, only to reveal closure at last. The latest variation is to wear one's trousers cata-strophically low-slung, as though they had seconds before they fell down, while all that is revealed is shirt-tails and underwear. Again there is miming. The man seems to want to show his lower midriff and the top of his buttocks as plump girls do now – but he does not show it: he cannot.

When men and women models pose side by side, we see how little in practice the double-act of the genders has changed with modernity. In the photo in front of me, the girl exposes her fore-arms and her bust just as she could have done at any time since the mid-1700s. Her modern dress is knee-high, so we also see her legs, to the extent that we have been able to for nearly one hundred years. And we see only one garment, her dress. If she wears under-clothes, they are hidden as her intimate skin is hidden (although matters are freer than they were, and women may now show a bra-strap or a T-shirt under a looser top). The man by contrast wears three visible layers of clothing: an open jacket, unzipped, over a shirt that has both buttons and zip – both are open nearly half-way down – over the inescapable tall T-shirt. He wears stylish jeans, he has designer stubble, but in terms of covering and uncovering his body, he is exactly as much covered as he would have been in the nineteenth century, the eighteenth century, and the seventeenth century.

In short, men wear more clothes than women – and more layers of clothes, and looser clothes, with a greater weight of cloth – which they wrap closer round them. What is it that men are trying to tell us? Is it that they feel the cold more? But if so, why do they keep unfastening their fastenings? One could say, I suppose, that all these unzippings, undoings and open-necked shirts, are proofs of relaxation, even of trust. They show the male warrior unlatching his armour, disabling his shields and guards. Perhaps, if men are aggressive underneath, they need to do this. Maybe too these shows of easy openness go with a sexual self-contentment, with the male complacency that lets men sit with their legs well apart in a way that women have been too modest to do.

Or perhaps men only pretend to be at ease. For their perpetual last resort of covering their skin – their reluctance to let more than a fraction of it show – could also seem distinctly worried. As if there were an unease at the core of masculinity about the relationship between the body and sight. Modern man is not Mark Antony. And modern man may have several anxieties. For men must prove their manhood both to women and to other men, while within they may be afraid of failure, afraid of emotion, afraid of women, and – the *coup de grace* – afraid of fear. Men do not get frightened.

It does seem that the world has divided hopes of men. It wants them to be at ease and relaxed, not rigid and frigid and uptight. And it expects them to wear at least two layers of covering. If a man wore to a formal event a garment that showed his skin in the way that women show theirs, we would be disoriented, even shocked. This is certainly the effect of some lively designs by Vivienne Westwood. In one, a swarthy and virile-looking man paces towards us wearing a little number made of brightly coloured ostrich feathers, exposing his chest and almost all of his bare and reasonably muscular arms. Even apart from the feathers this figure is startling because he is doing, on a smart occasion, what women do frequently and men do never: wearing a single garment over bare skin.

There may, of course, be a simple explanation for male shyness. Men have more body-hair than women, also men have stringy sinew where women have pleasant plumpnesses. But this cannot be the whole explanation because when men do uncover – in gyms and in the summer – they expose those places with most hair and sinew, their forearms and their legs. The world does not complain.

Or one might say that men dress according to a long tradition, whereby the clothes one wears, and even the weight of them, may represent authority, and the confidence that goes with authority. There is an age-old symbolism whereby ample cloth reflects worth and importance, or the weight of the office into which one has stepped. People with clear authority, such as judges, have been layered in over-garments, as kings used to be, and as the pope and archbishops still are. Women's skirts have also been big, it is true, and have sometimes trailed along the ground. So perhaps it is especially when clothes weigh on the shoulders that they represent responsible power. A man, or a politician, takes off his jacket when he means to show he will get down to work. But it may also be that when men – or professional women – put their jackets on, and with pleasure fit them snugly about their shoulders, they are putting on visible responsibility, and a confidence to match.

It occurs to me that I should look further at shoulders. It was a crucial stage in women's unveiling of their bodies, when they came to uncover their shoulders. And for men the uncovering of the shoulders has been extremely fraught, if not impossible. Even Mark Antony's shoulders had been covered by his "tunica". The issue arose again, more than a thousand years after Mark Antony, when the mutineers of the Bounty were in the South Sea Islands, and were to be presented to the paramount chief Arapeea. For before the chief, all men must bare their shoulders. But for Fletcher Christian and his fellow-officers it was unthinkable for a gentleman and an officer – even in mutiny – to bare his shoulders. A solution was eventually found, by manipulating pieces of native embroidery, but the problem had seemed most grave. Even now male shoulders are among the least exposed parts of the body, and in muscle-building courses, as in the construction of super-heroes for Hollywood, special emphasis seems to go to accumulating shoulder-pads of muscle-tissue, as though, in the last resort, muscles were an additional form of clothing. As perhaps they are, psychologically speaking.

For women too the issue of shoulders can be sensitive. In around 1900 the painter John Singer Sargent caused a furore when he showed his portrait of "Madame X" with one slender strap hanging down off the shoulder. The strap was scarcely more than a thread, but loosening it was a step too far, and Sargent was required to mend the portrait, and replace the strap. Only later still could shoulders be wholly naked. It is as if exposing the shoulder were nearly the ultimate exposure of body, or as if, actually, the human shoulder were the most seductive treasure the body offers to desire.

It is beyond my remit, however, to try to fathom the mystery of shoulders. In general, one important motive for covering the body is sexual modesty. Freud tended to treat any body-covering as a symbolic extension of the basic form of human dress, which covered the genitals. Freud would add that in protecting the body from sight we are protecting it from fingering hands, since sight is a hands-off form of touching. But not all body parts are symbolically sexual, and it would be surreally weird to call shoulders genital. Shoulders can, nonetheless, be shapely, delicate and beautifully fine for all their sinew, with a lovely balance of mobile bone and plumpness. One might think that, with their hills and hollows, shoulders are an especially difficult and interesting part of the body for sculptors, and the sculptor Henry Moore, in some of his most abstract works, seems still to be remembering the different moulding contour-lines that may be softly traced on shoulders.

There is no surprise if shoulders are often covered, since so many of our garments hang from the shoulders. If we did not have shoulders it would be harder to wear clothes. But since shoulders are so often covered, they may also look, when exposed, extremely vulnerable, even though they also are the nexus of the body's strength, the hinge of the arms, which for fighting men do everything, and which for most of us do nearly everything. It is their capacity and mobility that makes them vitally important; and it is because of their importance that we guard them anxiously, and also feel most tenderly for them if they should be exposed. Most forms of metal armour have protected men's shoulders, while the limbs, as in the ancient world, have often been bare. It is perhaps by exposing their shoulders, in their lovely and often fragrant beauty, that women show how extremely far they are from the warrior world of male aggression.

To return to the broad question of why men are so covered, the fundamental point perhaps is that – however individual our clothes may be – still our clothes are the image of our social persona, and our gender persona as well. Then the way in which men's dress is closer fitting and more covering than women's would go with the way in which the male persona is more contained and constrained than the female persona. Our maleness, our masculinity, sits on us more closely, wraps us round more economically, than femaleness does our partner. This shows in bodily movements too, both in fashion photos and in any photos. Women more easily raise their limbs, or stretch their arms to the full extent. Men seem more circumscribed, as perhaps they are in their feelings also.

I dare say this is no bad thing: not that either style is better, but because it is natural and good for the genders to differ, and compliment each other. In formal dancing, from the flamenco to Fred Astaire and Ginger Rogers, there seems a fit contrast between the taut, contained, hyper-energetic movements of the black-and-white male and the gracefully hurled limbs, and swirling fabrics, of the colourful woman dancer. The point about men and women seems to be that they *should* be different. But the difference in persona, which is reflected in clothing, has not always been as it is. Forget Mark Antony. If we go back to Shakespeare's time, we find the world was already different. Then, men's clothes had several features that we associate now with women: in the liking for silk and satin and lace, in the use of strong colours, in the taste for embroidery, cosmetics and jewellery. And men had features of character that now are expected more in women. The young braves in *Romeo and Juliet*, for instance, are distinctly in touch with their feminine side. They are man enough when it comes to sword-play, killing and dying, but also they are emotional and sentimental. The lead character falls in and out of mooning love at the drop of a hat, and his best friend amuses his fellow-bravos with fancy-free speech about fairies. The Elizabethan male persona was not emotionally contained as modern man is, as we can see from any string of sonnets. Prince Hamlet, again, is good with a sword, and can play the ironic philosopher. But he can also behave like a moody girl and easily gets hysterical. The painter Delacroix used a woman to pose for Hamlet, and on stage he is sometimes, aptly, played by an actress.

Then, over the next two hundred years, men did become more tautly disciplined. They came to operate with a more narrowly focused energy, which doubtless helped them to cooperate, and work more as one, in winning and holding new empires, new businesses, new technologies. To an extent men became more like good soldiers, more amenable to tactical regimentation, and soldiers themselves were changing through this period. In the late Middle Ages an army had been more like a rampage of hooligans, bravely dressed and with feathers in their hats, brandishing a miscellany of spikes, choppers and cudgels. By the eighteenth century, armies wore uniforms, drilled by marching in step, and fought with a synchronized firing of muskets, before, all in time, they fixed bayonets and stabbed.

In any event, men changed. In England we can see the change in the work of Jane Austen, because she loved Shakespeare's comedies and learned from them how to make her plots. And her heroines are like Shakespeare's heroines, or at least they resemble the clever, funny ones, like Rosalind in *As You Like It*, who is emotional and strong as well as clever, and can get away with pretending to be a young man. Although they are clever, full-hearted and strong, Jane Austen's heroines could not pretend so easily to be young men, not only because young women had become more ladylike, but also because young men had changed. Jane Austen's young men are not like Shakespeare's; if anything, they are more like Shakespeare's old men. They are wise beyond their years, make measured statements soberly, and presumably are meant to make good husbands because they are already like good fathers. They are especially good at managing: estates, parishes, families. If they are not like this, then they are rakes and scapegraces, but the rakes are as restricted, emotionally, as the pensive young heroes. And all this is so, even though, in Jane Austen's time, there had recently been a fashion for sentiment, and men as well as women were now supposed to drop a tear at the sight of a ruin or sunset. So it seems to me one may say that men's manners and passions were now more contained, as their bodies were contained in figure-fitting coats, and thigh-fitting breeches or skin-tight pantaloons, all of which were plain in style, sharp in cut, limited in colour, and without feminine, or Elizabethan, fripperies, such as embroideries, parti-coloured clothes or lace. The new men were masculine, smart and resolute. They could easily be dashing, but there was a narrowness.

It may seem odd to say that Elizabethan men were less tautly contained than later men, when Elizabethan men were just as much covered up as men at any later time. But so were Elizabethan women. Nor were the clothes of either women or men tautly tailored and sparing of cloth in the way that men's clothes later came to be. The Elizabethan period was a bad time for women's rights, even with a queen on the throne: but even so it seems that the male persona, and the female persona, were closer then than they later became. Perhaps a court culture helped this to be so, for it does seem that the leisured young men and the leisured young women at court spent a lot of time together singing madrigals, dancing in complicated patterns, writing and reciting sonnets, and in general giving careful attention to each other. In any event, it was easier for Elizabeth to compare herself to a man, when speaking patriotically, than it could have been for Queen Victoria. Over the two centuries between the two queens, the differences between female and male persona did become more schematic, in a way that shows in their clothes.

One could say that in these changes, men were leading the way into the future – into the region where we live now – in that an economically streamlined persona, focused on a public purpose, is the career-ideal now for both men and women. That persona is well "suited" in the modern closely fitting two- or three-piece suit, narrow and tubular but definitely elegant, with its single fabric and single colour to go with its single, focused purpose. The suit evolved in menswear, but may now be worn by women too since it is at once smart and professional. If we put the suit back on its hanger, and talk about the general use of trousers and jeans, that again is a super-trend led by menswear. Indeed all forms of "unisex" clothing – dungarees, tracksuits and jumpsuits, short trousers and short-sleeved shirts – are men's styles in origin that are now worn also by women.

At the same time it is clear that most women do not wear trousers, jackets or any form of unisex clothing all the time. Both at work and in leisure women operate a greater variety of clothes than men do. In the office or the boardroom a woman may wear a keenly moulded power suit, then a T-shirt and shorts or tracksuit in the gym, and later on a pencil skirt, or a full-length dress, or a travelling breeze of chiffon petals. When she wants, she may wear a blouse with leg-of-mutton sleeves or with no sleeves, or a dress with a sleeve on one side and not on the other, or open much of the way at the front or all of the way at the back. Her freedom to expose her body when she wants to is not compromised by her freedom to wear masculine coverings whenever she wants to do that also. It may be that many women's designs have something of the "retro", repeating with variations skirt shapes, bodice shapes and sleeve shapes from the past, but these old shapes are carried to new extremes of design of which the past could never have dreamed. So an empire-line profile can dance at the same party with bell-billowed skirts, sacks, pyjamas, flapper-type shifts and willowy black outfits that look like a cross between Bloody Mary and Morticia Addams – as it were the Queen of the Vampires who, it is true, will probably find among the black-suited men one with a chalk face, mascara and black-gelled spikes of hair, her Vampire Prince. But her white long arms and her bust may be bare, while his, invariably, will be hidden.

I do not want to simplify, and it is obvious, from the variety of very different styles that co-exist today, that both men and women have divided feelings about their clothes, and about their bodies, and about the extent to which they want the one to cover the other. Maybe it will always be so. But what is also clear is that these divisions are bigger and more momentous in women's wear. Nor do women forever cover, or uncover, the same parts of the body as they used to in the past. On the contrary the female body, and female dress, are like two partners in an astonishing dance across the recent decades, in which an important element is the exposing or hiding of different parts of the body in an irregular succession. It seems hardly to matter what part is uncovered or covered: arms, legs, one arm, one leg, back, bust, midriff, neck. What matters is the electricity generated by the constant surprise of new hidings and new showings, and in this process the familiar human body is forever restored to exciting new life. Because really the human body has few surprises: we know who we are and what we look like. Yet the effect of women's clothing, in its constant metamorphoses of fabric and body, is to translate woman into a magic creature or voluptuous elf who appears and disappears before us, forever changing and tantalizing.

The drama of menswear, by contrast, is not made of changing exposures and outlines. It is the drama of movement *within* a surface, a drama of sliding rucks and folds. What seems most important about men's suits, their tops and their trousers, is that the cloth should stay fairly close to the skin, but still be far from tight. In other words, men wear "second skin" clothes nearly all the time, only it is a loose skin, but then not too loose. If the layers of mens' clothing constantly part, it is only to show another layer beneath, while still, through the rhythm of coiling rucks, cloth signals body everywhere.

5. Team colours

We look for the clothes that are right for us, and normally, in the end, we find them. It is a little like finding the right pieces for a jigsaw puzzle. But finally we have an outfit, or a set of outfits, that are *us*. No one else will use quite the same combination: so we have a fabric "self", our show self for other people. Inside the clothes we have our private self, which we never declare entirely. We know, on the other hand, that our choice of clothes may give away some of our dreams.

Yet clothes are hardly individual things. They were more individual in the past, maybe, when tailors and dressmakers made garments to order. Nowadays almost all clothes come off the peg, mass-produced; and even in the past they were worked to a limited set of patterns. Perhaps too we do not want clothes to be *very* individual. We expect clothes to have something standard about them, to be recognizable as belonging to a known type or style of dress. In this way clothes help us to join with other people, however "personal" our choice of a blouse may be.

Clothes meet this double need, of being standard yet also individual, by being, each garment, in some way "special". Yet even the most special design in the store will have been manufactured, we know, by the thousand. If we were capricious we could imagine the most distinctive tops and skirts issuing from the factory gates in cohorts. Here an advance-guard of power suits marches, there – at two levels – trot the tops and the bottoms of the polka-dot bikinis, followed by a mist of iridescent camisoles, which make way sharply for the marathon stride, an avenue wide, of empty tubular straight-leg jeans. They divide in small groups and invade the stores, and separate again to find hangers of different sizes. Compressed, nearly hidden, they wait unchosen. All too soon the sell-by date arrives. Crumpled, dusty, they emerge, looking tacky now. Very few were sold. The unsold make their way to a discount store, where some find takers. Finally, with a sombre trudge, those that remain join the dreary multitude that drags, all colours and styles together, into the yawning landfill site. There they slowly degrade, into the petro-chemicals from which they were spun, with a needling toxic scent of death. That landfill site has choked; new pits must be dug.

So clothes – crowd clothes and designer specials – are mass-produced, then mass-destroyed. But if this occurs on an awesome scale now – awesome and horrendous – it is not in essence a new thing, for always clothes have had much to do with masses: with groups, and bigger groups, and super-groups. Clothes gather us and group us. Even royal robes in the past – scarlet cloth with ermine trim – grouped the royals of Europe in their own select paddock. The quality wore silks and velvets, which declared, from side to side of the continent, that they *were* the quality. Dustmen and coal-heavers wore hats with brims that trailed down their backs. Priests wore cassocks. Women wore skirts and men wore hose. The old wore gowns, the young showed figure.

If clothes group us, it is because we want to be grouped. For when we wear clothes, we are no longer alone: we have put on *member-ship*, we conjure a shadow force at our back. It may be an ethnic force, a race; or a social class, or an income-bracket; or a religious faith, with a further, supernatural force hovering on slow wings overhead, to guarantee protection in the next world as in this. In clothes we escape the vulnerability of the totally lone individual.

One could say that when we put on clothes, we put on gener-ality. Or that we put on an identity, since identity too is not a very individual thing. Our identity is made of overlapping generalities:

race, gender, age, class, politics. And if clothes make us safe within some big group, they also allow us to make micro-adjustments as to exactly where we stand. With a dissenting scarf, or tie, or cap, we can show how far we are from the centre of the group. It seems we have an inner dial that, within limits, we can turn towards greater uniformity or towards idiosyncrasy. In this way, with clothes, we can mark our singularity, even as our clothes, in their general style, make us safe in a group of groups.

Nor do clothes merely make us safe, for in giving us safety they may give us power. Wearing the clothes of any large group, we have put on a form of collective force. A power suit may dramatize the power of an executive, or of one who would be an executive. But many clothes are power clothes. Expensive clothes show money power, which is always galling to see if one's own resources are light. In the past, the very grand wore clothes that showed their grandeur, with trains that other people needed to carry, and perhaps with further people going ahead with staffs, to clear the rabble from their path. Our style now is different, when even government ministers and senior civil servants wear suits that they may have bought in Marks and Spencer. Others again will be dressed in Saville Row, and in the world of men collective power still quietly shows in a certain pitch of tailoring.

Uniform dress signifies power, although not necessarily authority. For the uniform may be worn by those who serve a power, as well as by those who exercise it, as is the case in armies. Or the uniform may be worn by those who serve, while those giving the orders dress as they like, as is the case in any restaurant. Or the same uniform may have a dual character, meaning power to some and service to others. Perhaps all power clothes have this ambiguity. The police uniform may inspire fear in the illegal migrant or the sidling junky: and it may seem merely the livery of service to the wealthy householder who vaguely smiles to the passing constable as he gets into his 4×4.

With the police we come to actual uniforms, and to a true uniformity in dress. Then, we may feel, we confront a uniformity not only of clothes, but of persons within the clothes. Not that uniformity of dress necessarily swamps the individual. In any small group in identical clothes – men in dinner jackets, a platoon of soldiers – the sameness in the clothes shows up their differences: how one is a tall, another stout, while a third has bow-legs. And the smarter the uniform – like those officers of hussars, who kick their heels on the fringes of nineteenth-century novels – the more aware we may be of a tension between the doeskin, in its tremor of tightness, and the fiery, unpredictable character within them.

In larger numbers, however, singularity dies, crushed by replication in the tramping regiment. Massed uniforms merge individuals into a greater, more unscrupulous agent, like those Indian gods with innumerable limbs. If it is our army, parading to a blaring band, then again we may feel that it is our strength we see, although it is the soldiers, not we, who wear the uniform. But if someone else's army invades our streets, then we know the terror of the power, which identical clothes help give to men. No soldier is single, and the sight of a face in the shadow of a helmet will not guarantee our safety.

Same clothes may mass men into a monster. Of course uniforms cannot be wholly to blame. The uniforms were not the origin of evil, if we go to an extreme case like the German SS: the Nazi party had reasons to seek to terrorize the nation. But Himmler meant the black uniform to awaken fear in every heart. And it may be that the smartness of that black-and-silver outfit, perfect in its impersonality, did assist recruits of humble background to act with murderous ruthlessness.

Group styles, in extreme situations, can mean death: death suffered and death inflicted. This may happen in war, with armies; and it may also happen on a smaller scale, and then on a daily basis. Recently in Iraq, a young woman reported, she was waiting at a bus stop when she saw a young Islamic extremist accelerate his motorbike towards her. She knew he was an Islamist because he was dressed all in black: and she knew he meant to kill her because she was wearing Western clothes, when the Islamists required her to wear an *abaya*. Fortunately his ardour was greater than his road skills: he came flying from his motor-bike and she got away. Since then, she always wears the person-covering *abaya* when she goes out. Every woman does, or they are dead. And you know who will kill you: the clothes they are wearing tell you so. The clothes you are wearing are their motive.

In the UK too – as the incident in Stubbylee Park, Lancashire, showed – it is possible to be killed simply for dressing in an unwelcome fashion. But at least in the UK there is no sanctioned and piously uniformed group that will kill us for wearing what we should not. Indeed, there is scarcely a uniformed force, beyond the police and traffic wardens. Even our armies seem only to wear uniforms to say Happy Birthday to the Queen – and then they wear antiquarian gear, busbies and scarlet. Mostly our soldiers wait, or sprint and fire and duck, in camouflage dress. Camouflage clothes loom large in our culture, as real uniforms, and frock coats, used once to do. Even children wear pyjamas with camouflage patterns. A man's suit has a good element of camouflage, since similar suits may be worn by those in very different ranks in a company, or an administration.

Clothes do not seem, at the present time, to be flaunted as banners of a group's superiority, or used as utensils of class-antagonism, in the extravagant way that obtained in the past. Both the rich, and celebrities, may "dress down" in casual wear, and even the Queen "dresses down" compared to any monarch before her, since the most distinctive mark of her royalty is that she always wears a hat out of doors. The very hatlessness of modern life is a form of camouflage, since in the past people used to wear their rank on their heads. Well-to-do men wore tall hats, and well-to-do women wore hats like trays, where humming-birds nested in flowers and feathers.

Even our generals today wear a sort of flat-cap, where Napoleon and Wellington wore hats like hills, set low on their brows like a giant's frown.

The same applies internationally. In nineteenth-century drawings and daguerreotypes of empire the colonial types strut in a solemnity of power. But dollar- and euro-imperialism have a different style now: laid-back and quietly suited. At home too leadership – even premiership – has changed its tone. We know well enough that power is power, with a formidable secret-service backup, although all we see is a friendly man in a charcoal suit – with blow-dried hair – who will be the prime minister. For hierarchy is camouflaged. Our model of the social group is the team, and we are all in the team so we should not look too different, playing within the rules on the level field of egality.

There has always been team power, of course, even in societies more openly hierarchical. Henry V invokes team feeling in Shakespeare, when he calls his soldiers, on the eve of Agincourt, "we band of brothers". He may be a king, but he is also a brother. He is a good team captain, as he shows when he tours the campfires at night, chatting with his soldiers like any soldier. To do this he will be wearing the same clothes that they do, even if he flaunts a rampant lion on the battlefield. For team power is fellowly power; the captain has power as the perfect team member.

Perhaps authority has always been tempted to disguise itself. King Alfred got his ears boxed, and other monarchs have circulated incognito. Philip II of Spain used sometimes to hang about El Escorial looking nondescript, and being mistaken for any functionary. He did it well, and he was liked for doing it. But on other occasions he was the blackly magnificent show king, and through most of history team fellowship, like other forms of fellowship, has taken second place to the spectacle of rank. Even God sat on a jewelled throne, attending by deferring angels. Power spoke from on high, literally – from a raised chair – and power was robed.

The team model is different, for the captain is less an overlord than the first among equals. He may have no special insignia of captaincy, and will not wear a different uniform. Of course the real-life playing field is far from level, as incomes and influence are far from equal; all that is equal is a notion of rights, hard to translate into fair chances for all. But it is easy to see why the model of the team has been institutionalized in the past hundred years. For team membership overrides the old-style gatherings of clans and regions and warring bigotries and social classes with their knives out for each other's throats. And within the big team, we can all be in lesser teams, which may compete. On the sports field teams may come to blows: but games have rules, and in this way our addiction to combat is sanitized. In daily life too we are all in teams. Our office is a team, our company is a team and our division within the company is a team. Mental therapy and coming back from drugs depend on teamwork. Hospitals are teams, where wards may be divided into red and green teams. University departments are teams now, made to compete for the cash prize. For big bucks may ride on the games that teams play, and only one team can win the cup; but the losing teams must be good losers, for all games end in tears for someone. Our economy depends on teams competing for dear life. The West itself is a sort of big team, up against teams with different rules.

Not that in daily life we wear the team strip, for team colours are the play version of team culture: they are for the sports field and the school. They are the happy colours of simple souls – red, blue, green, yellow, white, clear and bright – reflecting the youthfulness of team culture. The colours are a metaphor for team competition, because red and green and blue and yellow all have equal value, and any of them could be exchanged for any other. We wouldn't wear such young colours in the daily grind of work: and in any case, in daily life, we will not look too different since all our teams make up the work team. There are variations of course from domain to domain. Finance teams will tend to suits, where creative teams tend away from them – and into jeans, or denim suits.

These matters are well understood in Japan. There, each child in a school is placed in a team, and is a Red or a Green or a Blue. For two years the child works, in all fields of endeavour, for the success of the Red or the Greens or the Blues. Then the teams are broken up, and the children are grouped quite differently, and each one is now a Purple or a Yellow or an Orange. Now, in all fields of endeavour, they work for the success of the Purples or the Yellows or the Oranges. So they learn that, wherever they work, they must work hard, and work for the team. It is a good method for making company people, although in the company they will no longer wear, or talk about, colours. Even so they may be competing as their ancestors used to compete – if the films of Akira Kurosawa are to be believed – in which the soldiers all look alike, except that those of one warlord all have red pennons on their backpacks, when those of the other warlord are all green or yellow.

Western schools are less schematic about it, but they understand that a part of their purpose is to steer the unruly forces of life into regulated competition: so everyone will strive to be a winner, and join a group that strives to win. As an incentive there are the new quasi-aristocracies, the elites: the hyper-groups entirely made of winners. And anyone can be a winner; nor are winners resented, any more than sports stars are, or other stars, such as film stars and rock stars. I suppose they are called stars because we like looking up to them: if they made it, others can. They show that hopes don't always fail, and they may be more likeable than people born to money. Some celebrities even operate a combination of charisma, charm and rapport so they seem as though they are succeeding in some way *for us*: they would take us with them if they could, and in any event they depend on our love. The relation of the rest of us to this sort of celebrity is perhaps like the relation of a team's supporters to the players: really the players are a remote elite, a tiny aggregate of expensive champions, but we cheer them on, as English rugby supporters cheer on Jonny Wilkinson. The expensive clothes of such celebrities are likely to be casual and open in style, so as to show they have no side. Their clothes are an easeful part of the show which, in friendship, they put on for us.

There are other elites, of course, with a greater dependence on unfair advantages, and they may dress more divisively, in *haute couture* items that softly mouth "exclusive" and "*You* can't afford it". There are also the low-visibility elites, which we half-know of and seldom see, except briefly through the darkened windows of cars, or in momentary glimpses when they pause by high windows. They perhaps control the game, although they do not make it obvious by wearing power suits, or showing in the obvious high-fashion places. They are too powerful to be other than discreet: darkly smart, the ultimate power-in-camouflage.

If we ask where trends and fashions fit in this world of teams and groups, then clearly those who are on trend make another kind of team and a would-be elite. To be on trend is more like winning than losing. Perhaps it is even a kind of false winning, so one feels like a winner although one has won nothing solid. But as society works – if not the sports field – to look like a winner is a kind of winning. And those who are on trend can at least feel that those who are off-trend are losers. Those who lead and set a trend have a fair claim to be called an elite, although I guess they may not be elite for long, although on the other hand the great designers and couturiers are given willy-nilly a special glory of celebrity. I guess too that the different styles of youth subculture have operated other sorts of team colours: black and dead white for goths, flaming red spikes for punks, and hoodies or 1960s' retro styles for different contemporary groupings. At times street styles may come to blows, and in a way that too is a sport, since they are fighting for the sake of fighting: for love of it, as it were.

I want to pause on the subject of colours, and the way we play them up then play them down. For strong colour is both an ancient and a permanent resource, with which to mark groups and also individuals. The point of strong colours is that they are essentially markers, because they are conspicuous and because no one is, in fact, red, green or blue. Other features of clothing stay close to nature: fabrics are woven of fibres like hair, clothes never depart too much from the body shape, many garments are in the general range of human off-browns. But colours – like bold patterns – are pure artifice, brought from outside nature to identify a group, or again to make an individual luminous.

There are intermediate points on the scale, of course: festivals where most people will want to be colourful, and countries where, in the brilliant sunlight, bright colours work very well on everyone. But a general colourfulness is a different thing from the serious group use of strong colour, which may divide a society – or a society's time – into separate blocks. It is apparent in the UK, for instance, how we keep colours away from the work world, except in the form of company uniforms, where again the colours must not be too bright. A not dark but sober blue, a green the colour of green baize doors: these are workable colours for company staff in the primary world of work and money. Then colours can rip in the leisure and sports worlds, and at the weekend and when clubbing.

Or men and women, as mega-groups, may be marked by their takes on colour, women favouring colour while men incline to sober hues. Yes, in the male fashion pages there will be the odd canary or crimson jumper, or emerald bow-tie, or even a tangerine duffle coat. Also in central London, or in the environs of an art college, you will see striking outfits: a Withnail-length coat made of leather, deep-skirted and tightly belted, with additional leather brackets like misplaced epaulettes, worn perhaps with a luminous blouse with ruffles. But even if, in the metropolis, men's fashions have taken giant strides – helped by elegant outlay of the "pink pound" – sharp colours are not the norm. The mass of men seem at ease in deeper hues, especially if they can be named after wines, like burgundy. Nor do the fashion pages for men push colour; they prefer to find glamour and style in deep grey, a brooding, smouldering, sexy ... grey. Perhaps it is because men are thought to love machines that the menswear lines steer yet once more for the metallic, to iron grey especially, and the different tones of steel plate, with platinum and aluminium at the festive end.

It is as if many men want to be the background to women. Many men, again, work only two knobs on culture's television, the brightness and the contrast controls, leaving colour-saturation to women. But women, too, use grey, and black and white, and the deeper more masculine blues, browns and khakis. Women, again, will do metallic, wearing kinds of chain mail, or antique silver paillettes. But also – in fashion photos at least – women wear turquoise and emerald, and mustard and purple, and deep iris blue, and luminous orange, and an extraordinary range of reds. Women's reds are much refined beyond scarlet and crimson: there is magenta, burnt sienna, mist-pink and shocking red. True, women's reds are mainly flower reds: rose, fuchsia, cyclamen (with the odd rogue vegetable, such as a dress in tomato-red acetate knit). Women also do bold patterns, again in striking colours, and many such are gross but many others are brilliant. So, one could say, who needs abstract art, when we have women's dresses around us; indeed, when a dress may actually reproduce, person-size, a Kandinsky? Men, by contrast, prefer thin stripes and herringbones, often in a subtle and monochrome range.

It must be said that this women's spectrum of stunning colour is much more to be seen in the fashion pages than it is to be met with in the street. Nor do I know where the parties – or the receptions – are, where one sees so many strong colours together, as one sees in the pages of magazines. But even if the real world of women's colour is more subdued than fashion's dream world, the strong colours of that dream world – of that virtual society that exists in permanent technicolour – are significant. For still women do like colours more, and like more to wear them, than men appear to do.

If one asks what women's colours *say*, one must be wary. It would be too easy to claim, as I would like to, that women's colours go with their range of strong feelings, feelings that may be freer than the feelings of men, as if colour saturation went with emotion saturation. Whether or not that is so, colour has other purposes, especially, of course, display. And women do make a spectacle of gender display that leaves far behind the show put on by many men. Their brilliant outfits could remind us of Veblen, writing in a time when, he believed, many women had little else to do besides putting on a show. But if that was so in Veblen's time, women's purposes must be different now, when women do have, precisely, so very much else to do.

It must also be true that if women do not now practise conspicuous consumption to show off their husband's wealth and standing, they do practise conspicuous consumption to show off their own success, standing and indeed wealth, since even accessories such as handbags can sell at more than a thousand pounds. The wearing of expensive clothes always announces the possession of money. But implying a fat pay-packet, or a fatter monthly salary, is not the only factor and, in sum – if one has eyes in one's head – one can only be glad that women, in gaining independent careers, have not run down the gender theatre.

But nor is the motive of gender display as clear as I have perhaps implied. I dare say one can argue that when a woman wears red – especially a strong red – she feels relaxed about the amount of attention she will get: she might not wear red on a more reserved day. If she wears a deep marine blue it may not be for show, so much as because she is deeply calm – even though the blue goes well with her eyes. And one can perhaps say that when women choose the colours that they will wear, they are aware of the match between their colours and their mood at the time, or of the change they want the colour to make to their mood, or again of the mood or aura they want to project to others. As against men, whose narrow range of colours may go with the fact that they are less interested in moods. But this may be my own narrowness showing, because I don't think of myself as having moods, or care if I feel depressed or "good", since I find it more comfortable to think all the time that I am simply busy. I don't know if men are gainers or losers, in not having a culture of moods and colours. I can see though that without moods it is easy simply to switch back and forth between feeling happy and feeling aggressive, which seems a limited choice.

It would be fanciful to say that testosterone is chiaroscuro, and oestrogen the rainbow. And in any case men in the past wore a good deal more of the rainbow, and there are new men now who incline the same way. Whatever the meanings of colours may be, the colour cultures of both men and women are the result of a sort of instinctive teamwork. But, as in a Japanese school, teams need in due course to be broken up, and colours to change, to make the better cooperation that allows individuals to join in societies.

***

Colours join groups into greater groups, and into the great groups that ride the centuries. It may even be that if we wear colours with a rich history they can help us to feel more fully, and even to be possessed by, the greater emotions and moods, such as festive delight, grief, serenity. There are, of course, different ranges of colour. There is the optical spectrum, which we see in the sky when the sun shines through rain. There are the primary colours for mixing paints – red, yellow and blue – and the primaries for mixing light – red, green and blue. Human culture, however, has other primaries, and works especially with red, white and black. The values that we give to these colours are arbitrary, so red in the West has been the colour of kings (and latterly of those who would overthrow kings) and also of cardinals, the princes of the church, while red in the East is the colour of brides. Even so, it does seem that there is something broadly positive in the varying values that are given to red. It may be that there is a special excitement that the red vibration gives to the optic nerve, a more energetic effect than comes from the vibration of deep sea blue. Red is worn by brides, it appears, not from any association with bridal sheets the next morning, but because red, in the East, is the colour of festive happiness. It is worn by others at weddings, and red drapes, red robes, red banners, red lanterns, seem all to say, with different accents, festivity. These values seem then not so different from the widespread use of red by women in the West, as the colour of dashing, spectacular clothes, as perhaps the best colour for making a "splash".

One can find other associations for red: with blood, most obviously, and sacrifice. There is the "Halt!" red of traffic lights, and the red (another royal red) of the Royal Mail. Also, the old British army were redcoats. It would be nice to think that the red coats reflected brave hearts, although it seems that red was also chosen because, at the relevant time, the dye madder was cheap. The red of radical politics is relatively recent: the earlier radical colour was green. But the red of the red flag seems, again, optimistic, even triumphal, as the red robes of kings had earlier been, before they knew where their group was headed. And it is hard to associate a strong red with misery, or with lassitude, or with deep grief. Red does seem by nature dynamic. According to reports of recent research, football teams win more games when they play in red strips. On motorways I see red cars when they pass me; I never seem to overtake them. And if a person wears all red clothes, it can seem they are in contact with some sort of richness, connected to an energy, feeling a deep pulse. D. H. Lawrence liked to imagine that if human life ever changed radically for the better, then men would be relaxed, and ripe, and playful, and musical, and would wear red trousers. And on some men, nowadays, one may see red trousers, although not often the strong red that Lawrence had in mind.

The case of black and white is different. Unlike red, both black and white may easily come to mean opposite things. This is perhaps because, unlike red, they both are at once a strong colour, and not a colour at all. In another sense perhaps they are all the colours, since mixing all the dyes makes a muddiness like black, and mixing all the lights makes white light. At all events both black and white can be rich, smart and privileged, and also they both can mean death. Also each of them can attach to men, and again to women. There are some big parallels. In the West, black is the colour of death, of mourning and of funerals, and also is a colour strongly used in menswear, while white is associated especially with women's wear. And in the East the colour of death, of funerals and of mourning, is white, and also – in India – white clothes and white marks on the face are reserved especially for men. In some countries in the West a woman may not want to wear black because it would make her look like a widow. For the same reason an Indian woman will not wear a white sari.

Not that one should exaggerate the symmetry. In the nineteenth century, men wore black, and women wore both white and colours (and sometimes smart black, without being widows): and in India men wear white, but may also wear colours, and women too wear colours. But still the black and white chessboard principle is widely applied in the world. So we like Dutch tiles, and this page is black and white, and opposing empires may opt for black or white. The Spanish and also the English empires went in a good deal for wearing black: while the French and Russian and Austro-Hungarian empires tended to white uniforms, white greatcoats and white tunics. The Russian aristocrats were called the Whites, and the tsar was known as the White Tsar.

Of these two colours it is black that has grown steadily ever more popular. "Black is back", both black and white T-shirts say, and black returns so often that when other colours arrive, they come in black's clothing. "Blue is the new black", a headline will say, or brown or purple will be the new black. But if black is now the fashion-colour *par excellence*, it has climbed slowly to its eminence, and carries a long back-story, or many interwoven back-stories together, which have given it an extraordinary incremental charge for a colour that at the outset meant simply death and bad vibrations. We may connect it with the occult, and we also know of its connection with the "dark side" of sexuality, bound – perhaps literally – in a black PVC straitjacket. We know too that black is slimming, and on young people especially may be smart, dashing and glamorous. Its connection with the church is old news now; black is no longer, I think, felt to be especially Christian, and if anything may be associated more with Islam. There is a continuing perverse flirtation with Nazi kitsch that means, on the other hand, that we know that the SS in the Third Reich wore black.

Above all we know that black has been a man's colour: there are many "men in black" in the contemporary media, of which, recently, Johnny Cash has been the best known. Behind them stand other poetic shadowed figures, such as Lord Byron, who often appeared in black, and behind all of them Prince Hamlet. This is individual black, dramatic and conspicuous. But black has also been for men a dominant colour of groups – groups varying from priesthoods to kamikaze pilots, and especially of professional groups, such as lawyers, teachers and doctors. Also black, trustworthy black – important black – has been something like a uniform of those who handle money. Young merchant bankers have worn sharp black suits, just as stockbrokers wore black jackets with pinstripe trousers, and as usurers and many merchants wore black gowns for several hundreds of years. The gentlemen who wore black in the nineteenth century were smart according to the latest fashion, and at the same time they wore the dignity of ages.

It is not a fully attractive history, because for all the glamour and the depth of black, black also reflected something solemn and severe in the authority that men wielded. That is, however, largely history now, for men have withdrawn within the black domain. Contemporary man will wrap himself not so much in midnight black, but rather in intriguing shadows: brooding greys between charcoal and iron. The jet-black mantle has passed to women, for although women wear colours, they also wear black without thinking that they will look like widows. Women's black picks up on male capability when it is worn in smart outfits at executive meetings, and in general in suits and outfits that say: professional expertise. On the other hand women have the little black dress, a form of garment that men never came up with in the near millennium of their black power. That little black dress illustrates the range, and the difference, of women's black. For although young men in smart black, and lovers in black, could be dramatic and magnetic, black never extended or flicked its bat-wings in such an absorbing spectacle as it has in women's fashions, with ever-increasing versatility down to the present moment.

Women's black comes in all shapes and moods. It may come in a taut suit; or in a mist of black chiffon; or in a person-sized muff of black fur, pinched to starvation at the waist; or in a lean long stride of black bell-bottoms. There are black-sequined corsets, black conical smocks, black Matrix coats and black suits like the male dinner jacket (although never were dinner jackets so slimly seductive). There are the black scarves, face-masks, cowls and pantaloons that are worn by women in Islamic countries. There is black satin, black silk, black velvet, black knitwear; black viscose, black rubber and black PVC. For different occasions there are black hats, black veils, black gloves, and flattering black pencil skirts. Also black underwear, black tights, and black shoes and boots. There is jewellery of jet and onyx, mascara for the eyes, and Biba used to do black lipstick. There is fun black and smart black and sad black and existential black; dancing black and bedroom black and sporting black and business black. There is devout black. There is self-assertive black, self-effacing black, and killer's black and cry-for-help black.

Very often, with black, there is a claim on our attention, for black easily makes an emphasis, in a mottled, dappled world that is far from black. The grief of black mourning is largely left behind, and black is likely to speak now, in some sense, of power, especially of an inner power brought to the surface, the power of the night which may also be the power of a gender. Black *was* especially for men; it is especially for women now. Even the littlest black dress has a radiation, like a small isotope. For black is not only elegant, it may be dangerous with desire. The French novelist Stendhal blamed himself, after the event, when he realized that the black dress that his friend had worn to meet him meant that she had been willing to sleep with him. But black also is ambiguous, and is liable to say, "If you wish, you may probe this darkness – the risk, and the reward, is yours".

I am speaking, I am sure, of dressed-up black, black with a point to make. There is also casual black, for the shapeless black parkas that everyone wears, which have become a failsafe garment. For there also is dull black and comatose black, and oh-not-again black in both menswear and womenswear, from which we turn away if our eye is not utterly dead.

And with all this said for black, still the top colour is white. White also, in recent history, has been very much a woman's colour, and in the nineteenth century especially was associated with virtue and innocence. So children and young women could wear white at a funeral, and in that century there were very many women in white. The white worn by girls was pristine and virginal, the cream-white of older women perhaps meant milk and mother's milk. White also played with women's skin-colour, which was close to white because seldom seen by the sun.

Virginal white goes further back. The Vestal Virgins in Rome wore white, as did priests and priestesses through the ancient world. But white was also a festive colour: the colour of happiness and celebration, to be worn at feasts, processions and parties. In ancient weddings everyone wore white, and this ancient use of white for men – for happy white bridegrooms and their relatives too – survives in Arab culture. The white robes that Lawrence of Arabia wears like wings in David Lean's film – and that make Peter O'Toole look like a figure of salvation for a benighted people – may seem odd since we know that, for their own reasons, the Bedouins and other desert peoples wear black. But David Lean is right: Lawrence did wear white because his host had presented him with the wedding robes and head-dress of a Bedouin bridegroom. He did so as a hint to Lawrence to get his life straight, given his interest in young Arab males. It is not clear how well Lawrence took the hint, but he liked the robes and wore them often.

White is practical too, and is a high-utility colour for low-lit places: Yorkshire coalminers used to wear it, however sooty they got; clowns and dancers often wore it on stage when stage lighting was poor; and whirling dervishes whirl still in white. Several European armies wore white in the eighteenth century (the French, the Swedes and the Austrians), when troops were hard to see in the gunpowder wars. But white was also a class colour, and while the Spanish court, and later the European middle class, were magnificent in black, the luxury white of the Austro-Hungarian and Russian aristocracies continued a use of top-people's white that runs back indirectly to the fine white woollen robes worn in ancient Egypt and Assyria. Since the true luxury white can be worn only once, it naturally signifies ultimate wealth. Again, in contemporary design, white vies with black as *the* prestige colour, and in modern architecture white trumps black.

If white was a power colour it could also be a terror colour. Sergei Eisenstein showed this well in his film *Alexander Nevsky*, where the cruel hordes of white-draped Teutonic Knights slaughter their way into Russia. We also know of terror-white from its use by the Klu

Klux Klan. The Klan, and Himmler's SS, are the terror extremes of white and black, and the Klan had been much interested in national socialism, and reproduced in its literature images of Hitler as a knight in shining white armour. The dark side of white is apparent too in its use in India, and further east, not only for shrouds but in general for the clothes, banners and drapes at a funeral. White is perhaps a natural colour for death, given that the dying may lose all colour, while bleached bones also are white. White is sinister and ambiguous in literature too, as in the huge, warm-blooded, death-dealing mystery of Melville's whale Moby Dick (and Captain Ahab would have worn white nankeen trousers, as well as a white whalebone leg). At the end of Thomas Pynchon's novel *Gravity's Rainbow*, which searches white and black to the darker depths, the perverted Nazi scientist Captain Blicero dresses his beloved Gottfried in ballet-dancer's white when he straps him, as the living payload, into the V2 rocket of his involuntary, bridal death.

Not that these associations are necessarily in play when men wear white shirts and sometimes white trousers, and women wear white tops, and skirts or trousers, today. The white angels have dissolved from sight in our empty light-blue sky. But white is clean and radiant anyway, and gives a bright tone both when worn by itself, and when worn with colours. And white symbolisms, like black, are easily woken. A fashion photo of a girl in the prow of a boat wearing white only, whether a beautiful white dress or a stylish white jacket and trousers, speeding before a merry breeze or even with a merry motor, awakens very easily the sense of a young life poignant with hopefulness. If our young daughter wears a lovely white dress, with white embroidery on it, her white brightens further with the girls' white of centuries. It may even be that she feels "not naughty". The white lab coat, on the other hand, has nothing to say morally, although it revives a metaphor that often props up morality, since it represents good washing, cleanliness, hygiene. On the sports ground, too, white is not just another colour. In football and baseball it is especially used by home teams, and presumably suggests the virtue and security of home. Perhaps, at the back of all such clothes there is an intuitive, and therefore permanent, symbolism

There can though be white irony too. At a certain point, Mark Twain, when he was old and famous, took to wearing all-white clothes all the time. He commissioned fourteen suits of white serge from his tailor, so he could wear a new one each day of the week while others were at the cleaner's. He called it his don't-give-a-damn suit, but although he lived in a sombrely clad New York, he came from the South, where the plantation owners wore suits of white cotton, and Southern styles, and slavery, had been large targets of his satire. His white had attack – he first wore it to testify to the Congressional Committee on Copyright – but it may have been white mourning too, for he was determined not to be morose in his grieving for the recent deaths of his wife and his daughter. He may also have been picking up on power white, for he had been impressed by the plain white suit of the Tsar when he met him in the Crimea. There may even have been a touch of blasphemous wit, since – although a profound sceptic – he did look in his white robes, with his hooked face and white mane, like a rogue Jehovah. In any event, since he lived in Fifth Avenue and walked out each day, his white suit renewed a steady challenge to the black suits all round him.

His white had a touch too of dandy white. In hot countries white is smart on dark skins, and may be focused to a sharpness of fashion. Men's white is dashing in Brazil, and in many tropical countries, and may be dashing too, though more rarely, in regions further north. Of our own contemporaries, Tom Wolfe is a white dandy. He is famous for his cutting white suits, and if you Google Tom Wolfe you will find him standing nonchalantly with a cane, or taking a tap-dancing tilt, in stylish white from top to toe. And his white is ironic, a look-at-me pantomime white within which the scathing satirist will deftly poke towards the dark side.

While white clothes, like black, may awaken the past, it is the combination of the two together – of black with white – that is most often seen now. Women may wear all-black or all-white outfits, but even more they wear outfits with large black-and-white contrasts: especially a white top with black skirt or trousers, or vice versa. Men may still, as they have for a long time, wear a white shirt inside their black suit, or a black shirt sometimes with white trousers. This basic contrast is as electric still as it was, say, in the seventeenth century, when many men and women wore black or dark clothes with a gleaming white cartwheel ruff at the neck.

But the combination, the contrast, throws out the old symbolisms. The more nearly one comes to an equal balance of black with white, the harder it is to associate either black or white with death or perversity or the sinister, or again with purity and virginal virtue. If black and white together symbolize anything, they symbolize human decision: the will to make the starkest contrast, the power of design as such. Against the world's medley of browns, greens and oranges, black-and-white says, "Here is clarity, here is identity". Outside the world of clothes, the combination of black with white is something like the signature of civilized economy. It is possible to argue about photography that the black-and-white image streamlines appearances, clarifying them into the essential image.

There are complications to the story. For instance, it is distinctive to men that they tend to wear black *outside* their white. Women wear white or black beside their visible skin. This brings us back to the double game of men, as if the white shirt, beneath the black coat, stood in for their skin, which still they hide. Or perhaps men's white shirts are their honour or honesty, beneath their dark coat of soiling trade.

Women too will wear white undergarments. They used to wear layers of white petticoats and underskirts beneath dark skirts and coloured skirts. Both genders, moreover, have shown an interest in wearing white below the waist. Men have worn white hose beneath dark doublets, or white breeches and hose beneath blue coats, or white flannels beneath blue blazers. Perhaps white clothes have a meliorative role, giving whiteness and goodness to the half of us that is closer to the animal kingdom. Not that I would press the point that white trousers make honest men of our lusty hairy legs. White or light trousers, of lightweight fabric, also feel good in summer. They seem to weigh less than other colours, their lightness, their light, gives us some lift.

But still it is not irrelevant to bring in animals. For if the black-and-white contrast seems one clear sign of human manufacture, humanity did not invent the contrast. Nor did the cosmos: the inanimate cosmos. Few elements in the periodic table are either jet black or snow white. It is otherwise in the animal kingdom. Darwin argues in his under-read second classic *The Descent of Man and Selection in Relation to Sex* that the superb glossy black of panthers and blackbirds had intensified from the primal brown through the competitive drama of sexual display. This has also bred the strongest possible black-and-white contrast in penguins and skunks and zebras and beetles: again creatures with no genetic connection, although they share the purpose of attracting, and recognizing, mates. This makes our design use of the black-and-white contrast fundamentally natural as well. "Black is back", say the headlines. But the black-and-white fashions do not come back because in some form they are always with us, since they connect with the greatest group of all: with the infinitude of living creatures whose primary purpose, when they foreground their singularity, is to locate and unite with a partner.

6. Couturiers and *objets d'art*

It is the essence of clothes that they are secondary things, that they make sense only with people inside them. But still they are real objects in their own right, whatever illusions may be rested in them. I want in this chapter to look at clothes as things, trusting that this aim is philosophical, since philosophers from Plato to Heidegger have contemplated the reality of things. What value should one set on a garment, before ever one wears it: when one turns it in one's hands inquiringly, attending to the feel of its fibre and its knit, and asks, "How *good* a thing is this?"

Clothes have, for instance, a human value, which may in part consist of a human cost: a cost in life to the person who made them, working perhaps in conditions of exploitation. This happens more easily because the makers and the wearers of the clothes now have no knowledge at all of each other, and may be the width of the world apart. It was not always so. Once, those who wore the clothes might have had a hand in making them. In the poorest homes there could be skinning and spinning, and knitting and sewing, and maybe weaving and crocheting, so the whole family was involved. The better-off spoke face to face to the tailor and the mantua-maker who clothed them.

Now virtually all our clothes are made by someone else, and we have small means of guessing who they may be. The price tells us nothing, and certainly a high price does not mean that a careful seamstress has been generously rewarded. For the price is – or is meant to be – a mirror to our appetite. If the price is high, it is in the belief that we ache to buy this exclusive item – and will *want* to pay a great deal for it. As to a very low price, we hardly know if that means slave-labour, or barely touched by human hands. Nor do the labels – "Made in the UK", "Made in Macau" – make it much clearer. The nineteenth century was already aware of this issue. Popular authors such as Thomas Hood obliged high society couples to know that the luxurious gown for their daughter's first ball had perhaps been sewn by a poor woman coughing blood in a crowded, low-lit attic. And nowadays the making hands may be those of a seriously underfed child, stooped low and putting his sight at risk. First world or third world, the rag trade has buried many millions of human cast-offs without a backward glance, or any sign or memory left of them.

It is not that working conditions have at all times everywhere been cruel. Through the nineteenth century conditions in the factories improved. In the 1890s the girls in the textile trades were making a name for showy spending and dressing loudly at weekends. They were perhaps the forerunners of the girls and youths who, in the 1960s, helped change the economics of fashion by spending fresh cash in Carnaby Street and Biba. These later young workers were not making clothes, however, and most people now who buy fast clothes as they buy fast food have not earned the wherewithal by making clothes themselves. As noted earlier, it almost seems in the nature of clothes that they should often be made by the extremely poor, for wages that keep them poor. The high street chains alleged to profit from the low pay of clothes makers include known names like Mothercare and Marks and Spencer, along with Tesco and Asda, but this, I guess, means that all of us profit from ruinous clothes pay, and both our cheapest clothes, and the clothes we like best, are in some sense bought at someone else's expense. One can blame the chains and the brands, and the government too, and say that New Labour is not helping true labour. But I suppose the government would act if it thought our votes were in it. It does seem that the fair trade movement has begun to have some effect on the linking of clothes shops to sweatshops. In the meantime, and for the present, there still is the situation that many clothes that cover our shame are themselves woven, if we but knew it, of shame.

As to the other element in the production process – design – we are now given with our clothes a name that claims to have conceived them. A name-tape may even be stitched to the cuff, where it used to hide behind the collar. Not that the name will be the person: Chanel cannot now be Chanel, nor Balenciaga Balenciaga, and Calvin Klein is most likely not Calvin. Nor do we know if the design team hovering behind the label has truly invented the style, or adapted it cleverly from somewhere else.

Design, however, belongs with the subtle question of aesthetics, and there are more basic issues as to how we value clothes. The first thing to say must be that most clothes have no value at all for us. Clothes can be ugly, vulgar and ridiculous. They can be uncomfortable, or hampering. The synthetic fibre may be slick as slime, with a suspicion that near a fire it would flare in toxic smoke. I have been sanguine in this book about the huge choice of clothes we have, which includes very many well-designed clothes. But that choice includes hordes of cliché clothes, which are almost identical to other hordes of clichés. There are innumerable dull designs, manufactured in even duller colours – endless gherkin greens crossed yet again with black. Other clothes seem feebly spun from reconstituted plastic, and likely to wear out before the weekend. There are countless clothes that say too much, with imbecile phrases stamped up-front, when they would be fine if they were a plain colour with no decoration.

Also there are past clothes that had value and lost it, not because the fabric perished, but because the style died. It is easy to be ironic about the way in which the same garment may be a priceless treasure one year and an absurdity ten years later. I would like to think both values are exaggerated: that all the time the item in question had a value of its own. But I am implicated in the seesaw changes when I look at my own clothes. I still have a black suit with flared trousers that I bought in the late 1960s. I cannot now imagine what that younger person was thinking when he thought that it looked good.

The values we set on clothes easily drop from them. It is true that the converse may also happen, and the unthinkable may jump into fashion. Ugliness is in the eye of the beholder, and – in the eye of an interesting beholder – can, with a blink, acquire intrigue. Jean-Paul Gaultier said, "It's always the badly dressed people who are the most interesting". Always, Jean-Paul? But one sees his point, and his own designs may walk a hairline between the stunning and the ridiculous. The painter Alan Davie has said that when he taught composition, he would ask his students to take the shapes of three numbers – say 2, 4 and 5 – and make the best design out of them that they could. The results were normally attractive, and insipid. Then he asked them to take the same three numbers and make the ugliest design they could. The results were normally more dramatic, more interesting and, in sum, better than the "good" designs. A torn blouse, a skirt made of cylinders, may be given a twist by Issey Miyake or Hussein Chalayan and suddenly find intrigue.

Which raises the question, where do values live? If value can arrive suddenly on a garment, and later abandon it totally, like a passing bird, we seem wholly at the mercy of caprice. In a way we know that values cannot be absolute. Things and acts have value *to* people; to others their value might be different, or nil. And this is especially so with aesthetic values. But even aesthetic values can acquire an emergent validity as people persuade each other to see things in a similar light. The problem with clothes is that they exist in an intermediate realm. They are affected by moral values: they can be decent or lewd. And they are affected by subtler considera-tion. For instance, do furs carry the blood-guilt of the sufferings of the animals? Or should furs be revived because the Inuit are suffering?

The difficulty is that values tend to come in separate families, such as ethical values, political values. There is not an inclusive science of the value of values. As far as clothes are concerned, however, one could perhaps begin with the basic materials of which clothes are made. For really clothes are made out of very few stuffs. Apart from animal skins, there are primarily wool, cotton, linen (i.e. flax) and silk; almost everything else is synthetic. About synthetics we have our doubts, just because they *are* synthethic. But the natural materials have an intrinsic value because they have stood us in good stead for so long. It is not a moral or an ethical value; decidedly not in the case of cotton, which used to profit from slavery, and still is bought, from third world growers, at near-starvation prices. But still cotton in its stunning whiteness – whether in hair-balls on the plant, or made up as muslin – seems somehow to be *a good thing*. Even more, wool and silk seem like value made tangible. Nor is this surprising since mankind has worked for centuries – or millennia – at refining the very best forms of these things.

It is not hard to say why silk is good: with its shine, and its smoothness, and because it takes colour beautifully, it seems already more than half way into aesthetic value. The finest wool smacks less of art, and seems more like quality made tangible. With wool one must include the fine hair from other animals, in addition to sheep: from goats especially, but rabbits and camels too. An acquaintance has a pashmina made from a fine cashmere said to come from the beards of a certain style of nanny-goat that thrives in the foothills of the Himalayas: so its story is romantic, but in any event it is, to the touch, wonderfully fine wool. The wife of a missionary to China once showed us, shyly, the wool lining of the silk jacket she had been given in China. It was an unbelievably delicate wool, minutely curled. It was, she said guiltily proudly, the wool of unborn lambs. Without going so far in our sourcing, we know the warm and slightly oily fineness of the purest, softest wool.

Manmade fibres have a shorter history, and need to work harder to seem "good things". The trade is working on them, however, and already "viscose" can come in fine, puckered, lightly textured weaves, with something silky to it but also a dry crispness which makes it good both to see and to feel. There are other synthetics that may seem so slithery, so close to being ectoplasm, that they feed our sense that modern life is losing substance, becoming light as a hologram, iridescent as a soap bubble. Early manmade fibres like rayon, which were made from cellulose and ultimately from plants, had sort of organic credentials. Nylon and its successors are more problematic, and we may all be at times uneasy about laying on our skin the plaited polymers of petrochemicals: they are not so much a good thing as an alien thing. This is confirmed in science-fiction films, where aliens of all shapes normally wear synthetics as if other planets could have no equivalent for the animal and vegetable fibres that we know, because such things are *ours*, and ripen beside our homes.

Not that we often encounter synthetics in their pure form, or the organic materials in *their* pure form. Many materials are a mix of fibres. The nineteenth century loved barège, a fine gauze mixed of silk and wool, and modern garments all state their percentage mix of angora with nylon, viscose with silk, cotton with elastane. Few garments are 100 per cent polyester. In this way virtue is spread. Nature is reinforced by artifice, and artifice loses its stigma by keeping good company. So chiffon seems woven of air and gossamer – that is, of the webs of tiny spiders – whether actually it is spun of silk or synthetics.

If we move from materials to made-up garments we enter the dangerous domain of fashion, and the risk of falling into vanity and folly. And almost all clothes are called "fashion" now, especially in colleges and bookshops; I guess "fashion" is a sexier word than "clothes". But still, there are kinds of clothes that live at a happy distance from fashion and folly, for instance, work clothes.

It would be hard to find either conceit or deceit in a well-designed, strongly sewn, durable pair of dungarees. The critics of clothes – like Socrates or Kant or Nietzsche – do seem especially to have their eye on the dandies. But most people are not dandies, and most clothes *are* work clothes. The twilled cotton fabric called "denim" (from Nîmes, where it was made) or "jean" (from Genoa, where it was shipped) gets its cachet, at the high end of the market, from the fact that it still looks like the tough work material that it was in the seventeenth century, when it was one of the materials that people called "fustian".

I remember – when I worked in a factory between school and college – being struck by the leather aprons that platers wore. The leather was necessarily strong because it had to stand constant rubbing against fresh-cut metal edges that might still have a burr. And it was supple, or worn to suppleness, by constant movement. Whether the platers applied dubbin to keep the leather "alive", I don't know. Maybe the fine vapour of machine-oil, which hung everywhere, did the job. I remember it as lustrous, deep-brown, wonderful leather.

At the high-practicality end, the combination of flexibility with strength looks like honesty, like a material form of good will. Obviously the point could be pushed to absurdity. Presumably a NASA spacesuit is a supremely well-designed and well-made garment, but if you need to go to the moon to put it to the test, you are outside the spectrum of appreciable human values. The same would have to be said of other well-made clothes that save us from extreme environments, such as the articulated metal armour some deep-sea divers wear, or the Kermel suits that guard you when you walk through a chemical fire.

More appreciable for us is the value of the heavy-duty clothing that the human race used once to wear. In Herman Melville's novel *Whitejacket* of 1850, the narrator finds an old, very well-used big linen shirt. It is just a shirt, but he takes it and mends it and quilts and stuffs it, and sews extra pockets all over it, until it becomes a form of mobile home for him, in which he does all his shipboard tasks, and still can climb the rigging. When he falls into the sea he does not drown because the quilting is so thick with air that the shirt becomes a life-jacket. On another fall, however, the quilting becomes water-logged, and makes a lead weight to drag him to the bottom. Then he has to work – and it is hard work – to cut himself free of his white jacket, which his companions mistake for a shark impatient to devour him.

The question is, what sort of linen was that? Flax is a tough plant, and clearly it can yield a sturdier yarn than we like to put now in our light summer shirts. In the past, as it were, linen *was* linen. Still, we do have our own heavy-duty clothes, which are not all work clothes. There is the whole outdoor market: clothes for walking up alps or skiing down them, or for hunting. They are to be found in shops that seem the vigorous opposite of the chiffon world of boutiques: rubbery, hard-coloured, hung with lamps and camping kettles, under bracing neon lights that remind you of keen winds. There, among the wellingtons and walking socks, the torches and the travel towels, one finds the true heavy-duty garments, of hollow-core fibres, fleece-lined and water-repellent, complete with underarm ventilation. Hunters are especially particular, I am reminded by the magazine *Guns and Ammo*. Hunters value scent-control, the warmth-to-weight ratio and the truly stealthy silence of synthetic low-nap knit materials, not to mention the extra pockets, suitable for a walking slaughterhouse. A good deal of hunting wear is synthetic now, but substantial too, giving some answer to Herman Melville's linen.

I guess, however, that the heavy-duty synthetics are not worn next to the hunter's skin. And mention of texture, weight and stuff must bring in the intimate question of feel. Because our world is so eye-obsessed we may not talk so much about feel, but even if we seldom talk about it, still, for nearly all our clothing, feel is close to everything. Our clothes are the closest companions we have; they touch us all day and perhaps all night. They are closer than our shadows, which lie at our feet or lean on nearby walls. We rub and pinch clothes before we try them on in shops, because their feel-good factor is literally that. However they look, they must also have a good feel if we are to feel good. Probably we do not go so far as the composer Richard Wagner, who could bear no other material but silk against his skin. But we understand: the smooth cool *silkiness* of silk is close to the absolute feelgood value. And on the other hand clothes do not need to give us a rash for us to feel that we cannot wear them. They only need to be a touch clammy or slithery, an atom too crisp or hairy, or to crackle with static, for us to want to be out of them. There is no aesthetics of touch, but there should be: and a dressmaker or a men's outfitter might be the person to construct one. There can be a beauty in the feel, at one's fingers' ends, of even an artificial fur as well as beauty for the eye.

Beauty finally must be the issue, and what "beauty" means when one talks about clothes. But – leaving such fundamental things as fabric and feel – there are perhaps other issues to consider, before one stands tall and talks about beauty. There are, for instance, the social issues that arise because our clothes are a participant in nearly all our behaviour. For economy's sake I shall take a single value that may exemplify the social behaviour of clothes: I mean their humour and wit.

It may seem odd to speak of clothes and wit. Can a jacket make a joke? Fashion victims, and fashion designers too, are often thought humourless. But what is one to say when Giorgio Armani has a girl wear a dark suit (a suit adapted from a man's suit, but which fits gracefully her curved woman's body) and lets her wear, within the jacket, a waistcoat (again gracefully fitted), and also lets her wear a tie – but with no shirt beneath it. So she does exactly what men do with ties – she tightens the soft knot round her neck – but also she does what women do with neckwear, which is to wind it round bare skin above a bare *décolletage*. A man would never do this with a tie, although when Armani's model does it, we see at once that her action is witty, elegant and feminine.

This is a dress joke, though with a gender point to make. Elegance is combined with fun in a way that often may happen with clothes. The humour may be broader, as when Vivienne Westwood builds a bustle into a contemporary outfit: and what a bustle, dressed in tartan, and so bulbous it seems like the dress equivalent of a seaside postcard about big bums. It makes fun of women's fashions, and perhaps of their bodies, and probably too of the men who like such things too simply. Or for a man she designs a jacket shaped like the exaggerated musculature of a fanatical body-builder, all crusted with glitter and tinsel. It mocks at once men, their bodies and their tendency to hide both behind their bodies and also behind their clothes.

Jean-Paul Gaultier is more whimsical and fantastical: he will dress men in zebra stripes of coloured silk velvet, and striped top hats like the cat in Dr Seuss. He will let two models stand on exaggerated platforms, sticking out their bellies till they touch, so that they seem to guy pregnancy, while their heads lean back and look tiny because their hair is so tight, each of them having two tight little buns that look like Mickey Mouse ears. When he is not clowning, still there is wit, as when he lets a tight-waisted dress of aluminium-ish silk flare out extravagantly over a froth of flounced chiffon petticoat with a little the look of a washing machine exploding.

The point is not that modern designers have caprice, but that it is in the nature of clothes, as something we put on and also perform, that we are likely to play with them as we use them, just as we play with words as we speak. Wit and humour are part of clothes because they are part of life. They are an important tactic because we instinctively like – we cannot hate, we may be attracted to – the person who makes us laugh. There are other social values that are attached more closely to clothes, such as grace and elegance. When we call a dress graceful, we mean it will be graceful when someone chooses to wear it gracefully. Similarly with elegance. When we call a suit elegant, we mean it would be elegant if Cary Grant were wearing it – even though, as Simmel argued – elegance is an impersonal thing. Elegance belongs especially to new clothes, which have not yet worn and bulged to our shape. But still we need the man in the clothes, nor would the man be so exactly "elegant" without the clothes.

Grace and elegance have a double character. They are both a union and a compromise at once between garment and person, and also between the impersonal and the personal. Also both words, "grace" and "elegance", apply to clothes but with an appeal to further values. It is different with the pure dress value of "chic". Chic is versatile. Only certain items can be graceful or elegant, but anything – even safety pins – can be chic. They can have high chic one day, and zero chic the next. For chic is the clothes value *par excellence*, it is as free-floating as fashion itself. This is partly a matter of novelty, an invaluable value that disappears overnight. Chic though is more elusive than novelty. It is the most unpredictable of values, since it depends on a lightning form of group consensus that needs to be visibly arbitrary to be sure it escapes from – precisely – predictability.

Faced with the will-o-the-wisp of chic, there is relief in coming finally to beauty: to Beauty. For beauty cannot wait longer, and the question of beauty raises the further question of what exactly clothes have to do with art. In a way it is obvious that clothes can be beautiful: of original design, of gorgeous materials, and so simply yet perfectly shaped that "beauty" must be the word. This was well recognized by the philosopher Santayana when he insisted, of the quality of beauty found in works of art, clothes and buildings, that "beauty is a value … this value is positive, it is the sense of the presence of something good" ([1896] 1961: 33). Yet the great majority of philosophers and aestheticians, and even the great clothes theorists, have been reluctant to speak of beauty when thinking about clothes. What they have been sure of, on the other hand, is that clothes, however fine they may be, are something different from art. In his great essay "The Philosophy of Fashion", Simmel dealt with this question by exaggerating the difference between art and "applied art", by which he meant dress and also domestic furnishings. The look of clothes could not be called art, he suggested, because if we asked what art truly was, we thought of figures like Aeschylus, Shakespeare and Beethoven. This sounds persuasive: who would want a dress to be a tragedy? One might ask what would a Beethoven look like if somehow he had stumbled into the world of dress design? But he comes! The catwalk shakes to his tremendous tread, the model's face is ravaged and dark with power, while a surging tsunami of serge billows in thunderclouds above him, and pulses in the gale that is made by his stride like the elephant-beat of a gigantic heart.

But not all art is Beethoven or Aeschylus. There are sonnets and watercolours and light string quartets that seem less obviously incomparable with a startling and elegant dress. As to Shakespeare, we know from *King Lear* that he made clothes, and their removal, a part of his art. His heroines are forever dressing up as boys, Malvolio must wear cross-garters, Hamlet is the original Man in Black, and Macbeth finds that his stolen honours "hang loose about him like a giant's robe upon a dwarfish thief". As for Aeschylus, in the *Oresteia* the crucial on-stage mistake of Agamemnon is his decision – urged on by his ill-meaning wife – to tread upon a magnificent stretch of fabric. And if clothes and cloth are parts of the best literary art, they certainly are a part of art with any visual element to it. Theatre itself, and opera and ballet, are visual as well as musical forms, and costume is important to them. With regard to painting, clothes may be prominent in the Old Masters, and Titian may paint a blue leg-of-mutton sleeve with no less loving care than he gives to the wearer's face. A painting of a *fête galante* by Antoine Watteau may centre on the fragile grace of the rose and silver-blue satin *robe á la francaise* worn by a woman whose face we cannot see. True, the beauty of the picture is in the whole sweet-melancholy sense of transience that invests the silver-grey breeze-blown foliage as much as the elegant *robe*. But Watteau knew, as women may know by instinct, that clothes can match mood.

Nor is it a question just of textures and pigments. In baroque sculpture massively, as in baroque painting, ponderous capes and robes may swirl in soaring spirals. Again in baroque art, and in much art, the lift of robes, or their droop and fall, may "read" at once like the metaphor for a state of feeling. In Zhang Yimou's film *Hero* the same effect is seen when over-long red or white robes rise in an aerial dance like rolling emotion, borne up by wind-machines steered with art. In general in cinema – now also an art – clothes are important, from the tight jacket and big trousers of Charlie Chaplin to the scene in *American Gangster* where Denzil Washington betrays his drug wealth by wearing a chinchilla coat to the boxing.

The boundaries of art have moved since Simmel's time, in a way that makes it harder to argue that the design of clothes may not be art. The question is sensitive, however. There was some public unease and irony when the Royal Academy granted a massive retrospective exhibition to Giorgio Armani. Was Armani a Tintoretto? A Cezanne? It was essentially the same question that Simmel had asked, and obviously Armani is not a great oil painter.

The rag trade itself is nervous on this point, and sometimes tries to meet it by juxtaposing fashion with misery. So a dying man with AIDS may illustrate the United Colours of Benetton. So too we get fashion shoots deep in slums, or in wastelands of economic collapse, in early morning when the mist may make a delicate veil. There was heroin chic. All these things say: to juxtapose beauty with poverty and tragedy, that at least must be art, so fashion is art – and art with a social conscience, too.

There is nothing new in such contrasts. Cecil Beaton recalled how the designers of his youth would sometimes ask for photo shoots in the most poverty-stricken parts of East London. As he suggests, it was a gimmick then and it is a gimmick now. However Benetton may contribute to the AIDS campaign, there is a bad smell in making suffering the servant of fancy clothes. If there is an ethics of dress, these juxtapositions look like bad ethics.

But what then is the visual art of clothes? Not of clothes in paintings by Joshua Reynolds, but of clothes as such, freestanding outside the picture frame. One could perhaps begin with colour. In Chapter 5 I looked at colour, in the uniform of social groups. But team colours are hardly subtle colours, while actually the total range of the hues in clothes would support a searching aesthetics of colour. Both a painter and a dress designer might exclaim with equal relish "What a wonderful red!" over a particular magenta used in a painting or in a dress. Magenta is a deep colour, and perhaps not quite what Christian Dior meant when he called "the taste for subtle colours, the smartest of all tastes". But both in subtly powerful colours, and in the subtlest variations between grey and beige, textile colours are comparable to colours in oil paintings, which after all are normally laid on to fabric. Matisse himself, the master of early-Modernist colour, was inspired by the textile designs of the factories near his home.

The science or art – whichever it is – of combining colours is infinite in its possibilities. I remember, from my own limited experience of printmaking, the pleasure of finding – if one wanted to lay three colours together on a relief-etching – that it was hard to fail if one combined two strengths of one colour with one strength of the complimentary colour. As in red, pink and green, or red, strong green and light green. The eye likes the combination of recognition with contrast. But this is a basic choice: the remarkable harmonies are not so predictable. Beaton was astonished by the success of a colour combination used by the stage designer Léon Bakst: "mustard yellow, white, black, and emerald green – such a combination of colours as I would never have thought possible".

The art of combining colours is not entirely optical and abstract. Beaton emphasized his surprise by naming two of the colours mustard and emerald, and the thought of emeralds in mustard is viscerally unpleasant. If he had named all four colours after precious minerals, the combination would lose some shock. Colours have associations that affect the ways in which we like to combine them. Colours may also be invested with meaning, and this may be the area in which paintings leave clothes design behind. The poet and black-clad dandy Charles Baudelaire quietly worked for years at the question of why the colours in the paintings of Eugène Delacroix affected him so powerfully: now he compared them to musical chords; now he said the colours seemed in some sense to *think*. But the ways in which colours work on us have not yet been fully fathomed, and I can only suggest that an aesthetician of colour would ignore at his cost the long history of colours in textiles and clothes.

Otherwise, as to visual aesthetics, one might compare the grace of garments to the effect that an artist would get if he painted a light abstract on, say, a thin cotton, and then took a knife, cut a hole in the middle, and rested the work over the head of a friend. If he had liked the work before he might find that he also liked the different thing it had become, as the lines and colours swerved with the movements of the wearer. Clothes can be abstract art in motion, or figurative art, if the fabric shows, say, flowers. And if one says goodbye to the artist and simply cuts a hole in a rectangle of plain cloth, then, if it is draped over anyone's head, the folds and pleats will make good curves as the person moves. The unseen dressmaker here is gravity, which causes cloth, when hung between any two points, to fall in a graceful ellipse. The effect is the same if the cloth has a few straight lines marked on it: they will fall into attractive curves. From this point of view, clothes are geometry in motion, and some designers will mark on a dress the simplest rectangle of crossing lines, because those lines will turn to beauty when they curve as the body sways. It is a matter, in part, of laying regular curves on the not-regular curves of the human figure. What then seems to matter is that the curving fabric should approach the body in a changing way, now close now loose, and this applies both to trailing long dresses of women, and more finely to the cylinders and tubes that men wear. The person container must be now close, now loose. In the past women made a big play with close and loose, with their nipped-in bodices and flaring skirts. Men, in their reserved way, work the same effect, with their open coats and tailored trousers.

Soft geometry is surely one component of what one might call "beauty" in dress, the basic triad being body–geometry–movement. But whatever the principal issues may be, in the more abstract domains of dress aesthetics, there are many ways in which clothes design resembles the arts. When Dior describes in his autobiography how his New Look made its instant breakthrough worldwide, he sounds a little like those happy authors who quickly become popular because they have the gift of being both good and exactly in tune with their time. It may seem weird to compare a dress with a novel – like Carlyle comparing clothes to churches and national constitutions. Dior compares himself with poets and architects – he had wanted to be an architect, and clearly became one in cloth – and he describes nicely the "electric shock" of inspiration, when a new design "seems to hail you like a friend encountering you in the street".

The comparison with books may seem less odd when one thinks how different arts may achieve popularity because they offer a pose, a persona, that seems to many people to be the presentable "self" they have been looking for: a public face that answers to a private need or hunger. This may be a persona with whom many can identify, or it may be the persona of a dream partner. Lord Byron won such an iconic popularity at once for his sombre creations – his *Cain* and his *Corsair* – and for the stylish, accursed persona that he performed for a delightedly shocked society. Behind him stood Prince Hamlet, who gave a face and voice to an age that felt "sick at heart". And both Lord Byron and Prince Hamlet were not only a pose and a poetry, but also a dark suit of clothes.

The New Look is nothing like Hamlet or Lord Byron, but equally the New Look was more than a fashion. Dior speaks of the austere, unisex styles of the war years, and of the "Zazou" style, in which French women defied the Germans with big mops of hair on their foreheads. Dior said his aim was primarily to please, but he felt also that he was returning to women elements of femininity that had been eclipsed by the combination of modernity with the Second World War – a femininity for which, in the later 1940s, there was a nostalgic hunger. The New Look was conservative in its return to the low *décolletage*, the hand-span waist (as Dior called it) and the bell-like skirt. But the New Look came also with a sharp and stylish cut, and in some versions it showed more leg than the older spreading skirts had allowed. Within months the New Look was snapped up by stores from the United States to Japan, and across the world many women took to wearing it. The style had many variations, which Dior produced quickly, and it does seem that he met a need that went beyond clothes as such. He outlined a visible self, a kind of body to show and value, a kind of person one might want to be in the late 1940s and 1950s. In this sense Dior, producing sometimes two hundred drawings a day, resembles other prolific creative figures whose relationship with their public is a mutual inspiration because together they are responding to an emergent strong impulsion.

Dior said himself that he was reactionary, and his flower-women with hand-span waists have perhaps a less new look than the black-rectangle women of Chanel. To come to more recent times, the combination of the backward-looking and the forward-looking, which has marked many popular entertainers (including Shakespeare, Dickens and Steven Spielberg) – and which is perhaps inevitable in an ambitious artist who wants to please many – may be found again in the work of Giorgio Armani, our senior contemporary star at once of the catwalk and of the Royal Academy. Whether or not Armani is the Cézanne of design, he did respond in his way to changes that were occurring at the core of people, as to what it was to be a man and to be a woman.

Actually, that mammoth "retrospective" at the Royal Academy was misleading, because the visible emphasis fell on the high-society dresses that Armani has designed in recent decades. They are fine in their way, but his important originality had more to do with trousers and with jackets. When he was young he admired the way his mother – they were poorly off – made smartness from a plain skirt and jacket of his father's. One of his key moves, inspired by Marlene Dietrich as well as his mother, was to adapt the man's jacket so it truly could be worn with elegance by women, and not only the jacket, but the man's suit and trousers (for the suits of Chanel had continued the skirt). But already, before he did this, he had transformed the jacket itself. A famous film clip shows him shearing away the glued lining of a jacket, then losing patience and ripping out padding, interfacing, and all the internal scaffolding that used to make the male jacket erect, important, "tailored". Let it hang loose and graceful round a well-made youthful body! Then, having adapted the suit and jacket for women, he carried the soft ampleness of women's materials back into the fabric of men's suits and jackets. These changes were not made by Armani alone, but it was he, more than any other single designer, who decisively carried into clothes the changes that were occurring in the world at large: the erosion of old power divides, both between social classes, and also between men and women.

He was, of course, scarcely egalitarian. His new soft men's fabrics were often expensive special weaves, and his "power suit" was designed for a power body: for the executive toning his figure in the gym as he keeps a mean edge to company profits. Armani quickly became the dresser for stars collecting their Oscars, for he was good at combining luxury with tact, so as to help society's conspicuous winners to show how unaffected they still could be. Others of his men's styles seem especially designed for men who do not do much. His jackets and trousers drape especially well when worn with one's hands in one's pockets. Even in power suits his male models do not do more than stand about relaxed in an easy, kindly confidence.

In this they differ from Armani's women, who may pose with truculent thumbs in their pockets, or who may do things that his men would never do, like hugging themselves hard, or lifting one arm high to brandish a purse with a twist in the air. In one fashion photo his model, in her adapted man's jacket, eyeballs us with a lowered brow, pressing her hand to her lapel and her heart. Especially for women, he has done things with lapels. He gave one model's jacket a lapel on one side only, then folded it back again so it seemed like two lapels in one. The effect is vivacious and graceful at once.

At the same time he has carried the spaciousness of women's clothes into menswear. Menswear has often been taut, the male body moving within pliable pipes like a robot coated with cloth. But not, as a rule, in Armani outfits. An Armani jacket is like a hugely loose hide: and in giving men large, loose, ample clothes he has given them a space that maybe they have needed.

In general he moves wittily back and forth over borders. Sometimes his clothes are half inside out; one society dress consists of a mini-crinoline frame, which the model wears *outside* her chiffon. So for all his costly *de luxe* smartness there is a freedom in the way he makes opposites play. Women can take the suited stride of men, and men can move *inside* their clothes, rather than wear them like an outline. And his styles have come out in more afford-able versions, and not been confined to mega-rich celebrities.

Good designs are a sort of soft shell that suit what people feel they are fundamentally. Also designs can be a spark of life. I like very much a 1991 outfit by Issey Miyake (see Watson 2006: 305), even though I can hardly imagine on what occasion one would wear it. It is described as a "jacket of pewter silk plissé over chequer-board bloomer", and its colours are now brilliant, now subtle. The tautly poised model wears crimson tights and gloves, and a broad crimson stripe runs up her front as far as her breasts, where it gives way to a heart-shaped design in big chequered squares of crimson and light blue. Otherwise the thinly pleated outfit is a subtle grey-brown colour – perhaps one calls it "pewter" – with further patches of the same pale blue. The "bloomers" are short – they stop well above the knee – but they puff out broadly in a chequer-board pattern of grey-brown and a very light version of the same colour. I like the contrast between the way the tailored top fits her body so neatly and closely, while the bloomers, almost comically, balloon so loosely. I like the big schematic heart, which lightly says that she may have a heart, and which lets the crimson stripe remind us also of blood. The outfit is clearly designed for a young person who moves a lot. It looks theatrical, and would do for some sprightly part-supernatural figure, like Ariel in *The Tempest*, or for an actress playing a more contemporary Peter Pan. It has elegance, vivacity, originality, wit. It plays gender games, since the short baggy bloomers resemble the bulging trunk-hose that men once used to wear much more than any style of skirt, or even bloomers, ever worn by women. But also the bloomers suit women's hips, which are broader than men's. It is an outfit for someone taut with new dynamism, lightly playing, on occasion, with reminiscences of the old culture. As I say, I have no idea when one would wear it, but still I get a lift just from the sight of it.

As to what we wear at home – I should perhaps come home, at last – I suppose I feel the freshest pleasure, combined with the sense that this is art, when my wife emerges from a shop, or from a discount outlet, with a new coat or shawl or dress designed by Nicole Farhi. Farhi streamlines the forms, and there is something strikingly simple, original and elegant in all her designs, going still with a luxurious ampleness of attractive material, and an absence of decorative fiddle. In a coat that I especially like the lapel of artificial fur swings wide in a single, simple curve so that it looks like a standard lapel enlarged to the size of the coat; it is a brilliant design, simple and splendid.

So clothes are not a symphony, or an epic poem, or a drama by Shakespeare, yet still they can be art, and those who make them, artists. New designs can surprise with an absolute rightness, and a design may be right in several quite different ways at once, as unexpected good words in a poem are right. So clothes fit people and occasions too, including the most crucial kind of occasion. I have mentioned novels from time to time, and I shall close with an episode from a novel: one that shows how clothes may meet catastrophe.

There is a quietly tragic moment in George Eliot's novel *Middlemarch*. The town banker, Mr Bulstrode, is a severely Calvinistic puritan. But for all his moral self-righteousness, he has let himself help a blackmailer to die. It is perhaps the most convincing murder in fiction; he simply does not tell the old nurse, who is looking after the man who has been taken ill, that he should not be given the brandy that she wants to give him. In time the whole story comes out, and Bulstrode faces disgrace. But in his pride, and his puritanical privacy, he has said nothing of any of this to his wife. She is an extrovert woman, much given to ribbons and curls, but she rises to the occasion, and the way in which she meets it is by changing her clothes. I guess one must picture both her in her bonnets and ribbons and the dark, severe dresses of the old dissenting sects. She has gone upstairs, then George Eliot tell us:

She locked herself in her room ... She took off all her ornaments and put on a plain black gown, and instead of wearing her much-adorned cap and large bows of hair, she brushed her hair down and put on a plain bonnet-cap, which made her look suddenly like an early Methodist …

He raised his eyes with a little start and looked at her half amazed for a moment: her pale face, her changed, mourning dress, the trembling about her mouth, all said "I know"; and her hands and eyes rested gently on him. He burst out crying and they cried together, she sitting at his side.

Conclusion: dream clothes and future clothes

I ought, before ending, to return where I began: to the mistrust of clothes that has been expressed through history. One cannot say there is no reason for mistrust, for in all periods some clothes may serve vanity, and help disguise motives, and be produced in conditions of exploitation. Because clothes are an outer envelope that we can select and manipulate just as we wish, clothes probably always will serve as a powerful means and metaphor for various forms of misrepresentation. Yet still, on the subject of clothes, the wisdom of philosophy is incomplete; even, it has a blind spot. It may do the vain world good to hear Socrates say that the citizens of his (or Plato's) republic should go about "in summer for the most part unclad and unshod and in winter clothed and shod sufficiently", where "sufficiently" means "as simply as possible". That is a view. But the fair-weather nudism of Socrates hardly answers to the legitimate pleasure taken by many people – who are not vain or foolish – in fine materials, elegant designs, exquisite workmanship and beautiful decoration. Socrates goes on to contrast his simple style with the fever of urban luxury, with its "beauty-shop ladies", but these remarks simply clarify that underlying strain of misogyny that was to run through later philosophic thought on fashion, plaited in with a hostility to sensuous pleasure and to many forms of art.

As to the charge that clothes deal in false and vain appearances, one could retort that often – even mostly – clothes are simply part of the true appearance of normal humanity. We and our culture together have chosen them, our natures show through them every-where, and they do not necessarily mislead any more than do our gestures, our words or our expressions of face, all of which may be false or bad at times, although mostly they are not. Probably we can tell more about the inner nature of a person when we see them dressed than when we see them naked, because their clothes indi-cate – as their "honest" skin hardly can – many allegiances, sensi-tivities and foibles. To a great extent our appearance is our reality – and still we hold certain secrecies and privacies undeclared by any appearance.

In any case the old philosophic attack on clothes is heard less often now; nor do we so easily credit clothes, or even faces, with the power of disguise, since the development of psychology has given us new confidence that we can "read" the motives behind appearances. But something of the old mistrust survives, implicit in jibes about "fashion victims" and in the mocking tone often taken when naming labels such as, say, "Armani". The hostility is implicit in the word "fashion" itself, which is often used when the word "clothes" would do, precisely to cast a slur on clothes. At a lower but more immediate level, there is a hostility to fashion that can lead to murder, as it did in Lancashire. One might think – from the fashion pages in newspapers – that we live in a fashion-friendly world, but clothes have not lost their danger, or their ambiguity. Although some colleges teach fashion design now, formal aestheti-cians are wary of touching on the art of dress. And philosophy itself could be helpful here, not only because some philosophers – such as Erasmus and Santayana – have taken a more positive line, but also because the ingredients of a fuller appreciation of clothes are latent in many of the old severe arguments.

Immanuel Kant, for instance, had little good to say about clothes, but when he was talking about beauty in the world he distin-guished between what he called free beauty and accessory beauty. Free beauty is the beauty that any thing may have, regardless of its purpose. Accessory beauty is the functional beauty of any object that serves its purpose perfectly. He allows that the same object may have both kinds of beauty, for beauty is, it appears, in the eye of the beholder. So a flower has for most of us a wonderful *free* beauty because we love its form and colours without thinking why flowers exist. But for a botanist a flower has a functional beauty because every part of it is as it is in order to work as the reproductive organ of a plant. Kant allows that human artefacts may have both kinds of beauty. Rather drastically, he cites music with no words set to it as an example of free beauty, and the musical setting of a verbal text as an example of accessory beauty.

On such a basis one could, if one wished, celebrate clothes elaborately. There is debate as to whether clothes first began as adornment (that is, non-functional beauty) or as protective covering (which would be a practical form of beauty). What is clear is that clothes serve many purposes – both practical and social – which we are more or less aware of, while all cultures have sought to make clothes as attractive as they could. In other words, a single garment may combine several forms of both kinds of beauty. And if one allows that attractiveness for the purposes of reproduction is one kind of functional beauty – as it clearly is with flowers – then much of the free loveliness of clothes could even be thought utilitarian.

One must hope that, with time, aesthetics and philosophy too will open a little more generously towards the diverse beauties of clothes. It is not that clothes will cease to disguise or mislead. But beauty is beauty and – short-lived as clothes are – they live longer than flowers.

**

These last remarks have brought me to the huge topic of time, which I shall face directly in the time remaining. For clothes exist in time, and are at the mercy of time. Because of fashion, a particular outfit will often be the signature of a specific short period: a decade, a year, a "season". But also time is clothing's enemy, because fabrics are often delicate and vulnerable to decay. There are, however, realms where clothes do not change. It may be they do not change in heaven, for we cannot easily imagine how fashion should thrive there. There is also the realm of what should I suppose be called the social or cultural or communal imagination, where now we would locate heaven itself, and hell, if we no longer believe in them as destinations. And this realm is peopled with figures whom we recognize by their clothes. We know them also from pictures. They are a disparate community, for they would include, most sacredly, Jesus Christ, in his white loincloth, on the Cross, and also Jesus in white robes, preaching, while his mother, Mary, wears blue and red. There are figures of mythology, like Hercules in his lion skin, carrying a club. There are figures of national salvation, like Joan of Arc in clanking men's armour, with her pudding-basin coiffure; and embodiments of nationalist prejudice, like John Bull with his planet-shaped Union Jack waistcoat. There are symbolic political heroes, like Che Guevara with his beret; also family figures that are almost kitsch, like Father Christmas. Death makes flesh itself a form of clothing; in his strange, goblin way he seems the more sprightly because he has taken flesh off, and wears the ultimate nakedness of bones.

These figures live now because in life they made a big difference, or because they epitomize faiths and ideas, or because they are pivotal in regular festivals, or because they personify inescapable fears. Or they may live, for some centuries at least, because they reconcile contradictory hopes. So Robin Hood, in Lincoln green, stands at once for lawlessness and justice, also for aristocracy (as the Earl of Locksley), and at the same time for a free but basic life in the woods; also for feudal loyalty (to King Richard) and active revolt (against King John). His regular wear includes a quiver of arrows, which he uses to hunt for food, to show his sporting skill, and also to kill the enemy. He also embodies faithful love: for Marian, who likewise is both a lady and a rebel. Robin's Lincoln green supports local industry and is also a woodland green, although green was, in addition, the colour both of political radicalism and also of youth, Spring and May Day. Without the colour, and the hood, we would not feel we had all of Robin Hood, although he is also a master of disguise. Nor would he be complete if his band did not include Will Scarlet, in scarlet, or Friar Tuck, in the habit and tonsure that remind us that all England was Catholic once. I say this, having in mind that Robin's clothes and colours are fading, to judge from recent dramatizations: he remains nonetheless the original hoodie as hero.

There are other imaginary or fictional figures whom we know by their clothes: Peter Pan, another woodland rebel, is normally in green; Robinson Crusoe paces the shore in animal skins; Sherlock Holmes wears a deer-stalker; Miss Havisham sits for ever by candle-light, still wearing the crumbling yellowing remnants of her white bridal gown; Captain Ahab wears a black coat, with a white whale-bone leg. And all of these personages are fused with their clothes: when they appear in other dress, they are less than fully themselves. Hercules without his lion skin would be a berserk Irishman, brandishing a shillelagh: an impressive enough figure, and one with a stronger claim to historical authenticity.

In the domain of imagination, their clothes live with their life. In a more dispersed way, clothes live within the texture of language itself. For as the fundamental form of human covering, clothes have naturally provided language with one of its primary and most widespread metaphors, and language itself has been called the dress of thought. Since clothes *do* cover, these metaphors often incorporate suspicion, as with that wolf – forever on the prowl in the domain of the imaginary – with a sheep's fleece huddled close about him. But also Solomon in all his glory was not arrayed – dressed – as beautifully as are the lilies of the field. One might say that the long curved petals of lilies are hardly to be compared with clothes. But if all the world is the garment of God, then all of nature is the garment at once of the earth and of God also. And we would think of meadowland, stripped down to the clay for a housing development, as consisting for a time of "naked" earth. I only realized the strength of the metaphor of woodlands as clothing when a forest fire stripped the island that we visit in the summer, and the new landscape of crags, rocky earth, black ash and black stakes struck one as having a graveyard nakedness. I am aware too that, in writing this book, I have often slipped between speaking of real clothes and using metaphors that depend on clothes.

In this world outside time, of language and the imaginary, the oldest clothes exist unchanged alongside items as recent as Che Guevara's beret. In that realm clothes do not decay, and even the fig leaves of Adam and Eve, in the imaginary paradise, are a sort of ever-green. And Greensleeves is for ever our heart's delight. In the real world, clothes vanish. Those who wore them may have left a headstone, but the clothes they wore are less than dust now, less than air. And almost all of the clothes that the human race has ever worn have disappeared utterly: the pictures and descriptions that people made of them have survived much better than they have. Nonetheless, some clothes – real clothes – have survived, for one, or two, or even three hundred years. Having lasted so long, they may now last for ever. We can see them too, and almost wear them, mounted in museums and looking in unexpectedly good condition, as if the pleats in the muslin were recently sewn.

Such truly old clothes – worn in the time of Jane Austen, say – have a curious atmosphere when we visit them now, meticulously preserved, invisibly restored. It is partly because they are made by outmoded techniques, of yarn spun and woven by hand, with seams stitched by candlelight. But also they were once so close to their wearers that they are a little like ghosts. Pausing by them, we glimpse a vanished world: assembly rooms, nodding violinists, foursomes weaving in gavottes; the bows, the curtseys – eyes and shy laughter behind tremulous fans. Yet they are not ghosts, they do not suggest any individual, they have abandoned and forgotten utterly the people who wore them once. They are that other strange thing: old clothes.

Truly old clothes can have this odd double effect: they do, and do not, recall a past life. We have no such feeling about new clothes, in shop windows or on hangers. They have not yet joined humanity; the wearer is still to come, for whom they are lying in wait. Hopefully a young life will be inside them, laughter not veiled by a fluttering fan. But although the future *will* come, it has not come. There are no fore-ghosts of people yet to be. This is the big difference between gazing through time in one direction, and gazing in the other.

At times time itself seems woven in the fabric. New clothes are poised above innumerable maybe-futures, like the theory of parallel universes, whereas old clothes *are* the past, although clothes are also changed, in their nature and value, by the passage of time. Some items prove to be classics, they may even look better now than they did when new. Others were at the razor edge of fashion, and now they are fashion's grave. But then fashion reminds us that newness, too, is a value. Surprise is a value, a kind of waking up.

One may wonder what the future of clothes may be. I have been tempted to think, while writing this book, that we live in the future. As never before we have something like an infinite choice, both of new clothes and retro: it is a little like living in a utopia of clothes, especially if we compare our case with that of our great-grandparents, making the best of a limited set of bolts of cloth, pulled down off the shelves, and a small run of standard patterns. And it is interesting, if we have landed in the future, to look around and see how it is.

Because we know what the future was supposed to look like. In the past, people liked to imagine it. In Jules Verne, H. G. Wells, George Orwell, Arthur C. Clarke – in *Star Trek* as in *2001* – the future was envisaged in detail. Certain things were clear about it: for instance, that everyone would be wearing a lightweight leisure uniform, a streamlined jumpsuit of hyper-synthetics suitable for use on and off the starship. Unless, that is, one travelled *very* far into the future – say, several hundreds of thousands of years – when somehow one arrived back at time's other end. The blond baby-people in Wells's *Time Machine*, the ultimate young people in George Bernard Shaw's *Back to Methusaleh*, frolic in the simplest sort of Grecian tunic in front of a Sphinx or a temple with columns.

The imagined dress of the future resembled another sort of dream clothes: those worn in utopia itself. For in both the future, and also in utopia, fashion would appear to have been superseded: clothes achieve stasis and style rests. In the case of utopia this is hardly surprising, since utopias were mostly imagined by philosophers. One could perhaps say that the sewing-rooms of utopia are the one location in which philosophers are dress-designers. So it is no surprise that for Thomas More as for Plato the clothes of utopia should be rational, plain and uniform. In More's Utopia everyone wears plain leather for work, and wool in its natural colour when at leisure. The French *philosophes* in the eighteenth century were more exotic when they came to design ideal societies. In *Le Voyage philosophe* of Daniel Just de Villeneuve, clothes are made of salamander skin, and in El Dorado in Voltaire's *Candide* they are of butterfly wings, crystal and the down of hummingbirds. The eighteenth-century utopias glisten, which is perhaps to be expected of an age much in love with silk and satin. Their ideal clothes even sound futuristic. But whether of salamander's skin or of butterfly's wings, the clothes are standard in the given utopias.

Which is interesting since we know now, living in what would have been the future for H. G. Wells and his colleagues, and also in a kind of dress utopia – we know now that, so far from being uniform, clothes are infinitely variable. We are almost at the point where by punching a few keys, and touching a screen with a feather-finger, we can cause a new garment to issue from a machine. What then can the future be but yet more infinite variety and choice? Fashion lives, it will not die, and perhaps all we can guess about life one hundred or ten thousand years ahead is that still there will be fashions, and rapid change in the shape and the colour of clothes.

There will of course be new materials of which at present we can barely guess. It is possible to grow new tissue from tissue samples, and it may become possible to grow environmentally correct furs, the furs of fox and sable without the fox or sable in them, and high-grade leather without the cow. Or it may be possible to grow from tissue samples a sort of living fabric, kept moist and fed by micro-capillaries, but free from pain because lacking nerves. This hardly sounds like what we want. We are sufficiently ambivalent about our clothes without having clothes that come to life. One can imagine the horror movie where the heroine's living garment takes against her, and begins to squeeze like a million-fingered hand.

If one winces from what bio-technology may bring to the rag trade, there are other possibilities. Already there are fabrics made of fibre-optic threads that change colour with the ambient light. Viewing screens may become so flexible and wraparound that one can play a movie all around one's dress. Instead of using PowerPoint, public speakers could flash up bullet points on their shirts. Dress designs are already highly dynamic, with curving lines that seem charged with movement, but the lines could really move, or weave or tie bows or, again, with a twitch of the sensor, one could cause one's black outfit to flare violently in crimson, or sink calmly into deep-blue depths.

And in spite of all this, way into the future, the finest materials still may be fine wool, fine linen, fine cotton and silk. Or maybe suits will survive, and still, in the future, have zigzag lapels. But however clothes change or stay, still the process of choosing just what to wear may remain in all periods nerve-wracking, time-consuming and punctuated with delight.

But I am becoming light-headed with futurity. There is no knowing what will happen in the future. What will happen in women's clothes cannot be guessed, beyond the fact that a lot will happen. And as to men's clothes I shall close with a question-mark. Men have begun to show their bodies more. For many centuries they showed only their faces and hands, but the T-shirt has changed that. Easily now men show their forearms; in effect they have arrived where women were in the middle of the seventeenth century. Whether men will go further, to a male *décolletage*, to exposure of the shoulder, the midriff, the thigh, I cannot dare to imagine. And maybe men should *not* do those things, while women are doing them. For I cannot believe that the future will simply look like Mark Antony, strutting in the forum in his short shift before sailing east, to the bed of love and defeat. But who would have thought that a garment much like the Roman toga would be still worn by women and called a sari? All things turn round with time, and the wheel of fashion often turns quickest of all.

Further reading

For a keen-minded account of clothing issues, and the controversies surrounding them, see Elizabeth Wilson's *Adorned in Dreams* (2003). The books of Anne Hollander discuss fundamental clothing issues in a vivacious and open style: her *Sex and Suits* (1995) examines the different main purposes of men's styles, and women's styles, and her *Seeing through Clothes* (1993) is the classic study of relations between clothing, the art of painting and our changing picture of the human body. Another leading current writer on dress and fashion is Aileen Ribeiro. Her *Dress and Morality* (2003) gives a vivid account of the moral (and immoral) implications that each age has read into new styles of clothing, and her many books on the dress of particular periods are alive with telling detail – for instance, of the remarkable swings of style that may accompany political upheaval, as described in her *Fashion in the French Revolution* (1988). The fashion columnists in the press are often both sensitive and shrewd in their comments; see for instance the recent book by the *Observer* and *Vogue* journalist Justine Picardie, *My Mother's Wedding Dress* (2005). Of the several academic journals that now deal with clothing and fashion issues, *Fashion Theory* is notable for its illuminating particular studies, both historical and up to the minute, as well as for its careful theoretical analyses.

Of the classic older texts on clothing, I have mentioned Thomas Carlyle's *Sartor Resartus* ([1836] 2000) and Thorstein Veblen's *Theory of the Leisure Class* ([1899] 2007). Georg Simmel's essay "The Philosophy of Fashion" is rich in subtle insight, and may be found in *Simmel on Culture: Selected Writings*, edited by David Frisby and Mike Featherstone (1997). The pioneering psychological study is J. C. Flügel's *The Psychology of Clothes* (1930). The critical attitude towards dress and fashion taken by traditional philosophy is examined by Karen Hanson in her article "Dressing Down Dressing Up: The Philosophic Fear of Fashion", published in *Aesthetics in Feminist Perspective*, edited by Hilde Hein and Carolyn Korsmeyer (1993). A notable philosophical essay on the profound importance of appearances, including clothes, for human happiness is Curt John Ducasse's "The Art of Personal Beauty", reprinted in *The Philosophy of the Visual Arts*, edited by Philip Alperson (1992).

Information on the working and living conditions of those making clothes, or producing the raw materials for them, is most readily available these days on the internet, both in dedicated websites, and in press websites that continue to carry recent reports, such as www.guardian.co.uk/business/ethicalbusiness. The website of the International Fair Trade Association (IFAT) at www.ifat.org, is informative on circumstances worldwide, and on the partial progress that has so far been made towards better conditions.

References

Barthes, R. [1967] 1985. *The Fashion System*, M. Ward & R. Howard (trans.). London: Cape.

Beckett, S. 1931. *Proust*. London: Evergreen Books.

Carlyle, T. [1836] 2000. *Sartor Resartus*, R. L. Tarr (ed.). Berkeley, CA: University of California Press.

Ducasse, C. J. 1992. "The Art of Personal Beauty". In *The Philosophy of the Visual Arts*, P. Alperson (ed.), 619–24. Oxford: Oxford University Press.

Flügel, J. C. 1930. *The Psychology of Clothes*. London: Hogarth Press.

Hanson, K. 1993. "Dressing Down Dressing Up: The Philosophic Fear of Fashion". In *Aesthetics in Feminist Perspective*, H. Hein & C. Korsmeyer (eds), 229–41. Bloomington, IN: Indiana University Press.

Heidegger, M. [1959] 1971. *On the Way to Language*. New York: Harper & Row.

Hollander, A. 1993. *Seeing through Clothes*. Berkeley, CA: University of California Press.

Hollander, A. 1995. *Sex and Suits: The Evolution of Modern Dress*. New York: Kodansha International.

Nietzsche, F. [1886] 2003. *Beyond Good and Evil*, R. J. Hollingdale (trans.). Harmondsworth: Penguin.

Picardie, J. 2005. *My Mother's Wedding Dress: The Fabric of Our Lives*. London: Picador.

Ribeiro, A. 1988. *Fashion in the French Revolution*. London: Batsford.

Ribeiro, A. 2003. *Dress and Morality*. Oxford: Berg.

Santayana, G. [1896] 1961. *The Sense of Beauty: Being the Outlines of Aesthetic Theory*, W. G. Holzberger & H. J. Saatkamp, Jr. (eds). Cambridge, MA: MIT Press.

Simmel, G. 1997. "The Philosophy of Fashion". In *Simmel on Culture: Selected Writings*, D. Frisby & M. Featherstone (eds), 187–217. London: Sage.

Veblen, T. [1899] 2007. *The Theory of the Leisure Class*, M. Banta (ed.). Oxford: Oxford University Press.

Villeneuve, D. J. de 1761. *Le Voyageur philosophe dans un pays inconnu aux habitans de la terre*. Amsterdam.

Watson, L. 2006. *Twentieth Century Fashion*. London: Carlton Books.

Wilson, E. 2003. *Adorned in Dreams: Fashion and Modernity*. Piscataway, NJ: Rutgers University Press.

Index